AF477812

editor assistant: Stéphane Argillet

Special Thanks to

Juliette Soulez, Alban Barré, Stéphane May, Pierre Bal-Blanc & Blocnotes,
Parachute, Geneviève Cadieux, Guillaume Dumoulin & Le Magasin de Grenoble,
Béatrice Paillet & le FRAC Poitou Charente, Galerie Jennifer Flay, Galerie Air de Paris,
Marie-Laure Paretti & UR (Unlimited Responsability)

© ÉDITIONS DIS VOIR
3, RUE BEAUTREILLIS
75004 PARIS

ISBN 2 906 571 92 X

CONTEMPORARY PRACTICES

ART AS EXPERIENCE

this series edited by
DANIÈLE RIVIÈRE

in the same series

TECHNO: AN ARTISTIC AND POLITICAL LABORATORY OF THE PRESENT
Michel Gaillot
& Jean-Luc Nancy, Michel Maffesoli

SOUND AND THE VISUAL ARTS
Jean-Yves Bosseur

IN FAVOUR OF TODAY'S ART
François Dagognet

CLEMENT GREENBERG BETWEEN THE LINES
Thierry de Duve

CONTEMPORARY PRACTICES

ART AS EXPERIENCE

PAUL ARDENNE
PASCAL BEAUSSE
LAURENT GOUMARRE

CONTENTS

Experimenting with the real
Art and reality at the end of the twentieth century

"There are still a great many of us in the world who think that putting poetry and art in the exclusive service of an idea, however much that idea moves us to enthusiasm by itself, would be to condemn them in a very short time to being immobilized, and amount to sidetracking them." It was with these words that in 1935, at a time when avant-garde art was ossifying into militant sloganeering[1], André Breton blasted what had in the course of modernity become a common tendency: the yoking of artistic creation to a definite program. Between the lines, he was also suggesting that the principle of *experience* not be overlooked. Defying any illustrative function, creation is by its very essence seditious; it must open itself up to the possible, take on great airs, spill over in new directions. It must be driven by the experimental impulse because it mobilizes rather than immobilizes, because it determines an unappeased relationship to the real (in Breton's speech, a great deal was made of the real,

[1] André Breton, "Political Position of Today's Art", Lecture delivered by Breton to the "Leftist Front" in Prague, in *Manifestoes of Surrealism*, translated by Richard Seaver & Helen Lane (Ann Arbor: University of Michigan Press, 1969), p. 221.

and, consequently, of "realism" in art[2]). To argue for experience as a horizon amounts to defining an attitude whose relationship with reality is open ended.

If all art is the experience of something, it is nonetheless worth pointing out the varying degrees of experimentation involved. There is nothing in common, on this level, between the academy-accepted artist who perpetuates prevailing principles, and the avant-gardist, who is a partisan of the constant requalification of limits, in a libertarian sense. With the passing of time, however, as the excesses themselves inevitably end up being institutionalized and no longer exceeding anything much at all, art's experimental field narrows. The final moments of artistic modernity, between the 1960s and 1980s, may even be seen as establishing the sequence of experimentation either for nothing or for memory: Reinhardt treating himself to the thrills of the monochrome a half century after Rodtchenko; Bacon striking back out onto the via dolorosa of historical expressionism; Fluxus and actionism protracting futurism and Dada—though not always with the gift for transfiguration—and the list goes on. Not that everything has been done, as the commonplace, wielded with such dexterity by cynics and other sloths, would have it; nor that circumstances were the same, giving identical meaning to the same gestures. The fact remains: recurrent fixation on an already aestheticized object in quasi-mathematical fashion breeds plain, unadulterated fixation. Welcome to the hypocritical age of

---

[2] Unsurprisingly, Breton's lecture, on the *Political Position of Today's Art*, makes much of "realism" (this, after all, was the era of socialist realism) as well as of "realist art". Portions were devoted in particular to Courbet, herald of the genre, with Breton wondering aloud about the fact that the latter, who was a major player in the Paris Commune, never depicted it pictorially.

inertia passed off as movement, the age of copiers selling themselves off to the system under the guise of being pioneers.

The bitter end of the twentieth century in art can be qualified, at best, by contrasting practices, at worst, by their chaotic atomization. For this reason, any attempt to plot out subtle categories within its folds is a perilous exercise. Let us then resign ourselves, with all due regret, to simplifying.

On the one side of the field, in great numbers, one is liable to find the inevitable loafers; those who, as Courbet might have said, "live from death", rehashing forms long since worked over and out: "trans-avant-gardists" or "post-avant-gardists" of every stripe, experts in repeating history, masters of the post-figurative, the post-abstract or any number of other post-"body-art" schools. All of whom, occasionally, spruce up the sauces, or top off the whole works with a theoretical pastry that manages to perpetuate the illusion for a while longer.

On the other side, in rather less tightly thronged clutches, we find those whom it would be appropriate to consider as the authentically *active*—a disparate bunch, both in terms of their style and mode of expression, but federated by an intact introspective potential. These are artists for whom art is not necessarily about generating the "new"—the by-now somewhat time-withered watchword of the modernists—any more than it is about pretending to be something that it isn't. Artists whose approaches we will endeavor to analyze more closely in what follows—and above all the approach capable of running through our study like a guideline and providing it with the underpinnings of an identity: a position careful to hold reality up to its own standard, in step with and in the company of the real world, driven by the obstinacy to stay in sync with what's going on.

Experiri

The notion of "experience" (from the Latin *experientia*) stems from the term *experiri*, meaning "to try out". Experience, in its primary sense, refers to the process of actually going through something, a trial whose purpose includes broadening and enriching "the knowledge resulting from it"[3]. Through semantic derivation, experience also extends to the acquired practice of some activity as well as to the entire set of the mind's acquisitions resulting from the exercise of our faculties (John Dewey's classic "learning by doing"). Inasmuch as it is etymologically related to "experiment", it also encompasses, as is well known in scientific circles, the fact of actually provoking a phenomenon with the intention of studying it. Despite the extent of its usage, experience can be concentrated into one phenomenological principle: *the practical, theoretical and cognitive trying out of reality*. What is to be understood by that? First of all that reality, as a sum total of facts, ways of being, and, when one gets right down to it, of representations, is less a space that is known than a space to be experienced in terms of confrontation with a context. Secondly, that our position in this context, oscillating ceaselessly between activity and passivity, stems from an acquisition to be looked upon as a form of becoming. And finally that reality, which cannot be reduced to the principle of the given, actually provokes itself: it

---

[3] This definition can be verified in the Oxford dictionary.

being that which is and exists only to be infused, scrutinized, gone over in every direction.

Context, becoming, provocation. Drawing the portrait of the artist as an "experimenter", as a figure embodying the experience of reality, doubtless requires us to build upon this dynamic triangulation. The three-point model is less structured than it appears, and quite enticing: the world is an object for conquest, but it is also desperately backbreaking: as an object, the world is transitory. What the artist at the very tail-end of the twentieth century knows better than any of his predecessors—having given up on the feeling that art is by its very nature a major formula for human expression, or that it has the automatic power to set the forms of life   is that all experience is a *passing action.*

It is thus as a passing action that the art of the intimate, in full bloom at the century's end, is to be seen: an art measured against such daily experiences as washing oneself, making love, sharing a meal with friends, meeting someone—any number of circumstances which provide the settings for the works of Georges Tony Stoll, Rebecca Bournigault and Valérie Jouve, amongst so many others. Nothing short of a passing action is how those art forms based upon the random puncturing of the real, as substantiated with an occasionally stunning economy of pretension in the work of Martin Parr, as he photographs, one after the other, all the objects which now universally make up our contemporary McLives; in the work of Pierre Bismuth, accumulating in an exactly one-hour-long video-projection a thousand images of objects, things and situations which he has merely seen; or in the work of Beat Streuli, recording the stereotyped ballet of adolescent bodies in various metropolises across the planet whose lives are well on their way to cultural homogenization. In short, it is artistic experience—the gesture of introspection, of punctual questioning, of encounter taking precedence over form—that will stick with us. It is worth remembering, in this regard, the emblematic and prophetic *Scultura de passeggio* ("passing sculpture") with which, thirty years ago, Michelangelo Pistoletto covered the distance between three different Turin art galleries where he was showing simultaneously: the occasion for random encounter and a metaphor for art as a drive to be harnessed—fossilizing it as little as possible—as becoming. The mode of experience which was soon to be elected by many artists—in a common inflection in the direction of the authentic and the occasional—is to be found in the exploration of this in-between zone: what art has not yet sedimented, what experience is about to sediment in the yet-to-be-born form of the artwork.

A foothold in time

The "experimental" artist at the very end of the twentieth century is not actually an inventor of worlds. His is a way of not world-making, to paraphrase Nelson Goodman in reverse. Where does he come from, if not from a proliferating already-given? The central thesis in this matter is that of the *given world*. Notions of surveying, puncturing, observation, immersion all find consistent legitimacy—a factor of intense dynamism—in this full-world atmosphere. It is, as it turns out, the state of coexistence between a drive for aestheticization fed by no program whatsoever and a hypertrophied real world, accumulating in itself the unheard-of potential of what art can offer, which sets the art mechanism in motion. The artist? All he needs to do is to be there. The moment is always chosen, the *kairos*—that "opportune moment"—blends with *chronos*, the time of the slipping away of duration. A series of photographic works, such as Bruno Serralongue's *Concernant quelques événements de ces dernières années* [Regarding several events of these past few years], draws upon facts for which the artist was merely in attendance: a Johnny Hallyday concert in Las Vegas (*Destination Vegas*, 1996), or the restitution of Hong Kong to Red China (*Handover*, 1997). The odd and sundry as a constituent factor of aesthetics is in this case endlessly mirrored in that it is condemned to the walls of the art gallery or, as Pascal Beausse has put it with admirable subtlety, *"an inquiry into the real... a means of working at the crossroads of art and documentary, photography and information"*, where the artist, tackling head-on the notion of the constantly up-to-date, also *"tackles the particular context of fabricating images mediating reality"*[4]. Art, then, is a reactive practice. A reactive practice to be experienced in keeping with the economic model of *tense flux*, to employ the term Michel François once used to entitle one of his exhibitions which consisted of an accumulation of daily objects, press clippings, notes and lists of private experiences[5]. Between artist and world there is nothing but the breadth of a gaze cast here and now, nothing but the distance of immediate exchange. The law presiding over creation? Adaptation. And the artist's mode of presence? Staying in sync.

[4] Pascal Beausse, "Actualité de l'information ", *Bruno Serralongue* exhib. cat. (Corte: FRAC Corse, Spring 1998), p. 2.
[5] Michel François, *Flux tendu*, exhibition held at the Moulins albigeois, Albi, Summer 1998.

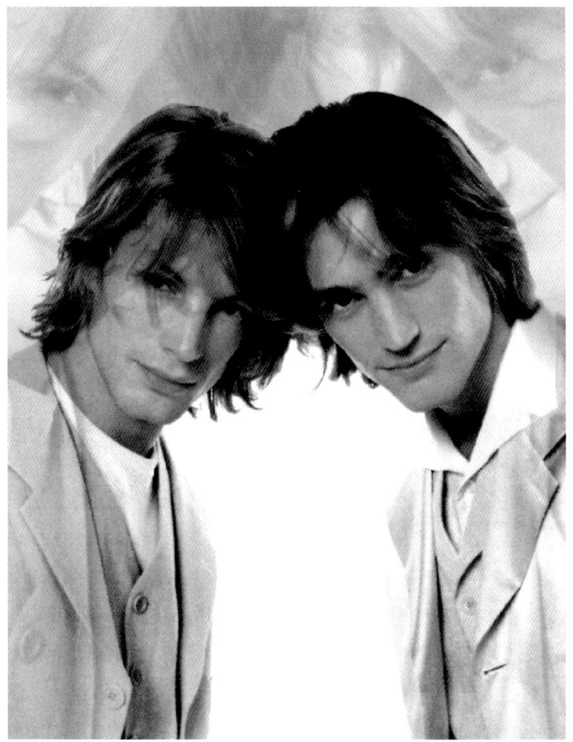

Claude Closky: *Les Cousins*, 1998
Video, 60 mn
Courtesy Galerie Jennifer Flay

Claude Closky: *De 1 à 1000 francs*, 1993 (detail)
paper and glass, 140 x 1350 cm
Collect. Centre Georges Pompidou, Musée National d'Art Moderne, Paris

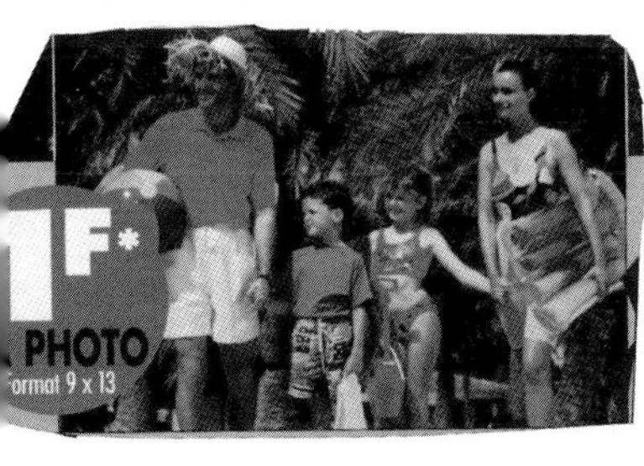

1F*
PHOTO
format 9 x 13

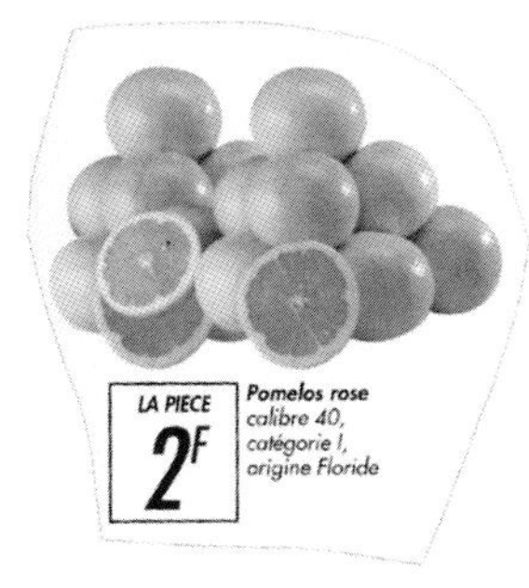

LA PIECE
2F
Pomelos rose
calibre 40,
catégorie I,
origine Floride

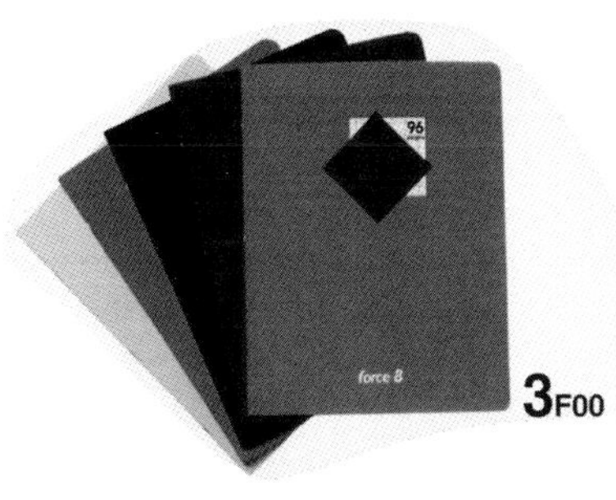

96
force 8
3F00

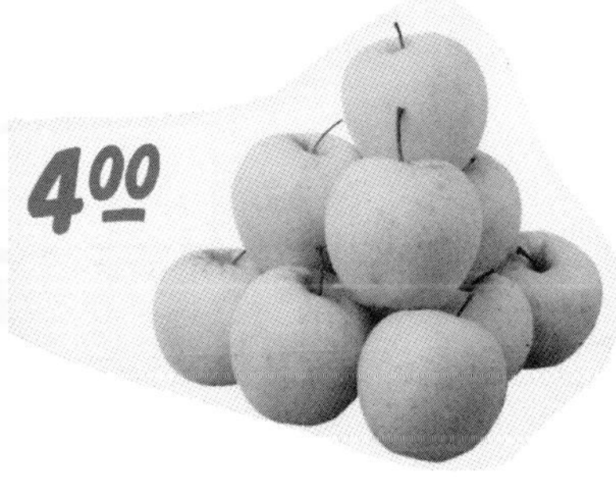

4,00

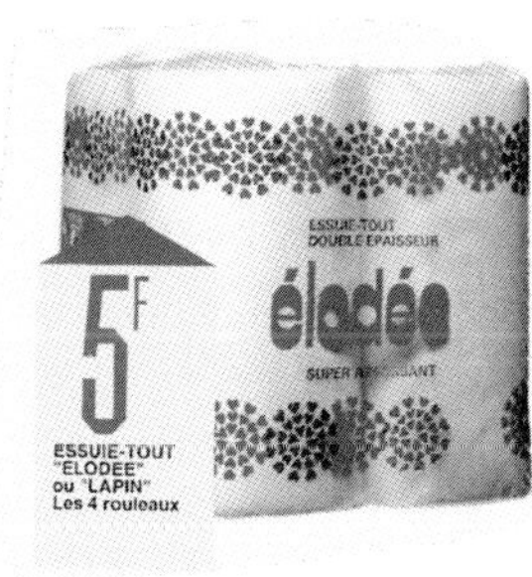

ESSUIE-TOUT
DOUBLE EPAISSEUR
élodéa
SUPER ABSORBANT
5F
ESSUIE-TOUT
"ELODEE"
ou "LAPIN"
Les 4 rouleaux

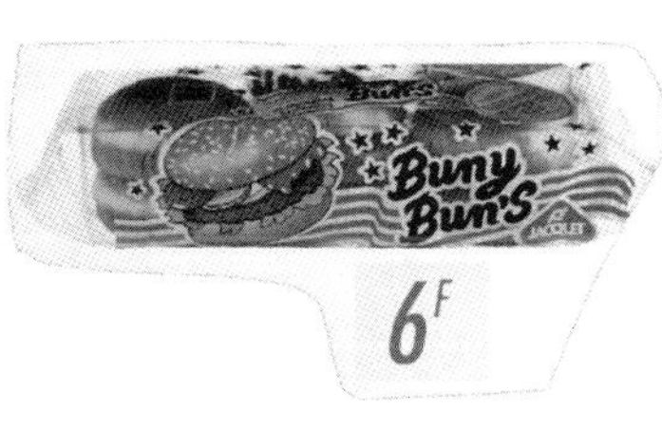

Buny
Bun'S
6F

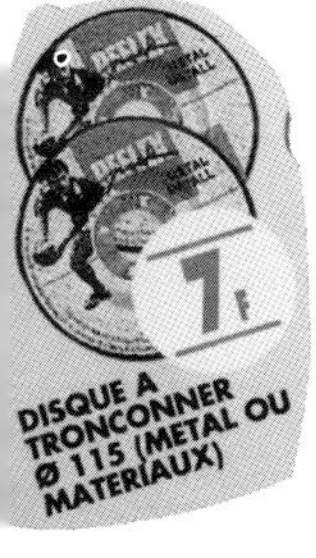

7F
DISQUE A
TRONCONNER
Ø 115 (METAL OU
MATERIAUX)

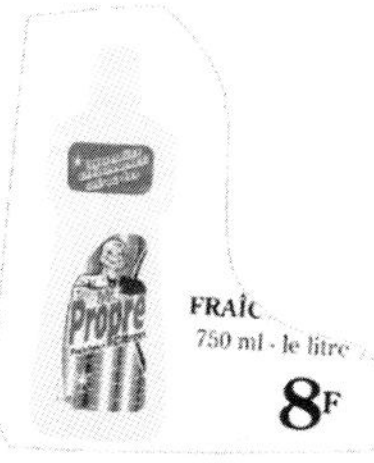

Propre
FRAÎC
750 ml - le litre
8F

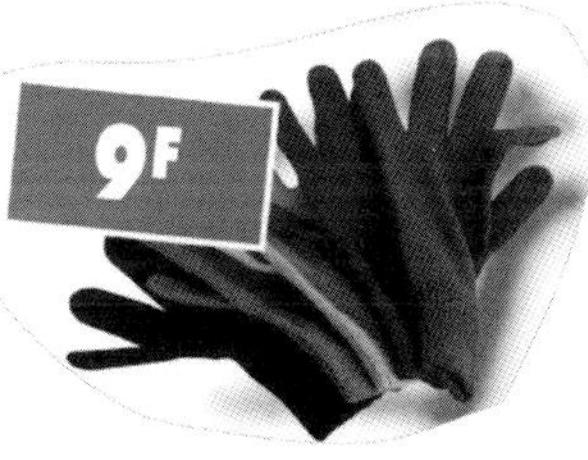

9F

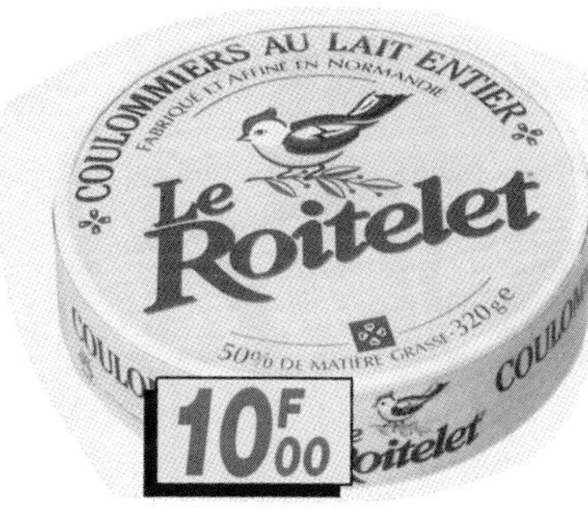

COULOMMIERS AU LAIT ENTIER
FABRIQUÉ ET AFFINÉ EN NORMANDIE
Le Roitelet
50% DE MATIÈRE GRASSE 320 g
10F00

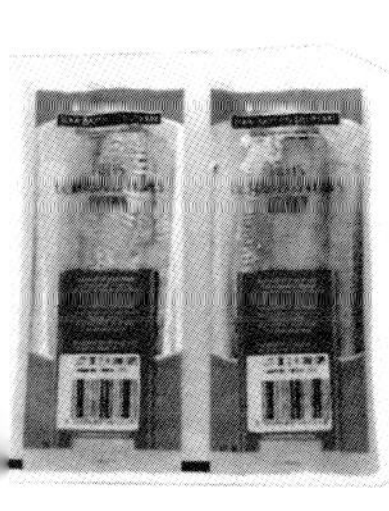
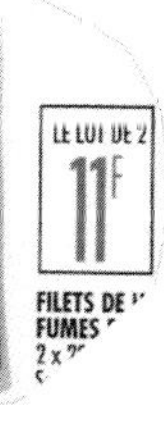

LE LOT DE 2
11F
FILETS DE
FUMES
2 x 2

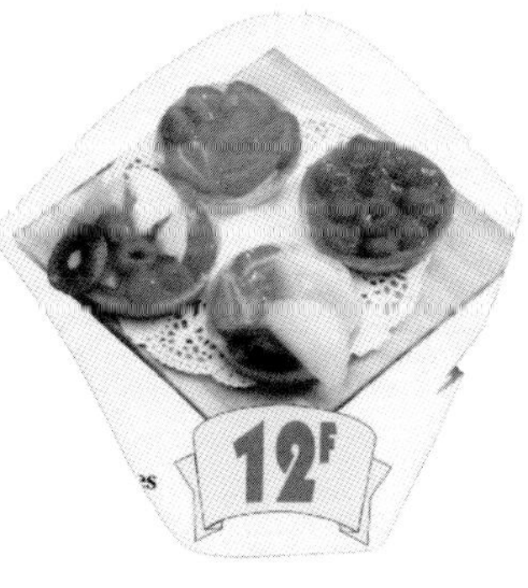

12F

POUDRE
ANTIPARASITAIRE
POUDRE INSECTICIDE
CAF
150 g
13,00F

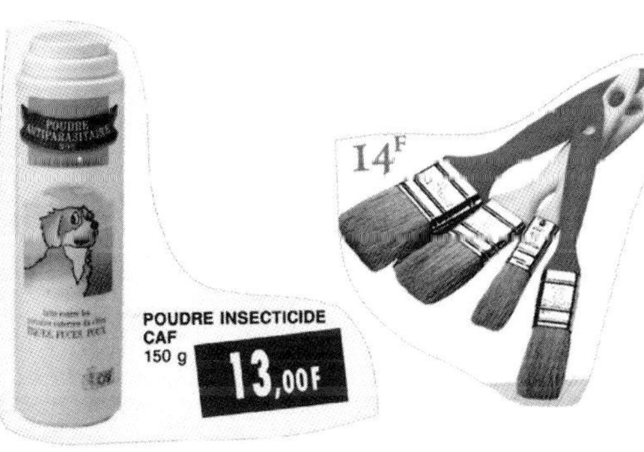

14F

Notions such as "adaptation" and being in and out of "sync" have, of course, since the very outset of the modern era, been central criteria for the analysis of art. The ways champions of the Old and champions of the Modern experience time are not in sync, though they live in the same world. As their degree of adaptation to reality varies, their artistic preoccupations are bound to differ, as are the aesthetic schemes that each propounds. Though this elementary bipartition has the advantage of clarity (those who espouse their era versus those who turn their back to it), it ceased to have any meaning with the advent of late modernity, generating the concept of the avant-garde (the future is better than the present), becoming thoroughly useless with the advent of postmodernity, favorable to a disjointed relationship with time (which involves *being there*, of course, but without any historical project). Late modernity, postmodernity: one as much as the other, in short, derails our relationship to the present. They mold a form of time consciousness in which both the notion of foundation as well as that of finality have withered; in which living in time comes down to wandering aimlessly through it, undergoing the traumatic experience of a disadaptation, of a loss of sync, of an impossible being in "sync" with a world hitherto thought of as in multisync.

Art, as a response to our aimless wandering in time, is determined in any number of ways: either as an escape (through the abandonment of idealism), or as a form of radical absence (interior experience), or even as an indexing enterprise (checklisting whatever there is). Everything, in other words, the last two artistic centuries, with extreme creative generosity, were so anxious to promote in bulk—though of course in the mode of an increasing dispersion, possibly giving the ambiguous impression that art itself is aimless wandering (an idea circulating between various modalities of experimenting with the present). The desire to be finished with such an ambiguity, one recalls, explains the birth, sometime about 1850, of an art decreeing itself to be "realist" (Courbet, Realism Pavilion, 1855), that is, wrenched free once and for all from the aestheticization of all temporalities other than those which were immediate. A hundred years later, it still had not lost the wherewithal to attract many very-late-twentieth-century artists to forms of art linked with the real—driven by the will for the occasionally millimetric presence of the real. This tension to aestheticize existence, to make *what is* the basis for art, is doubtless the result of a deficiency: when one gets right down to it, today, at a time when teleological ideologies and grand positive projects are all failing, reality is all there is left. It is the result, too, of the concern with "getting back in sync" implicit in any aestheticization of *what is*. Because ceasing to lose oneself in time demands full-time attention to the present; and requires, by extension, a form of proximity to beings in all their forms (people, objects, facts), which amounts to a return to the essential. Me *and* as well as me *in* the world. This "return to", in rejecting any centrifugal temptation, and in which the egotistical self must forget itself, does indeed stem from commitment—a particular form of commitment, whose aim it is to get back to the true proportion of things, to move back upstream to the moment of discovery which is at the same time the moment of taking stock of one's own position. As it happens, whereas modern commitment was political, and whereas postmodern commitment describes itself as being antipolitical, the commitment of artists toward the reality secreted by the end of the twentieth century can be seen as *antepolitical*. No prescribed will for organizing, no refusal of organizing either, just the desire to take the pulse of organization.

Puncturing the unrefined real

There is a tension in getting back to reality as it truly is. A sustenance in the order of things the world provides. In terms of art, the 1990s have shown that these attitudes are not exempt of radical thrust. Reality, in certain cases, will even be apprehended as a new object, a virginity, *upstream of any institution of anything whatsoever*.

Experimenting with reality in the crudest way, heedless of the structures which shape it, in a pragmatic rather than a rationally determined gesture, in an offering of the self to the acquired and directed against the innate. To become once again, in short, a "realist" artist in keeping with the previously mentioned criteria. Fine. One of the most troubling ironies of "realist" art in the second half of the twentieth century remains, however, *being out of sync*. Didn't New Realism, activated and theorized from 1959 on by Pierre Restany, borrow reality's most visible signs to constitute itself as art (Hains' and Villéglé's torn posters, Martial Raysse's appropriation of advertising iconography, Spoerri's relief paintings…)? Not entirely, because what was at issue there was a critical reconstitution more than an occasion for experimenting with reality in terms of what it actually was. Didn't the pop art of the early 1960s record reality in its most contemporary and most ordinary aspects? Yes, but it magnified them, lifting to the level of myth what the order of the real could conceive of only as a secularized, functional and banal form of the ordinary. Didn't the hyperrealist painters tagged as *photorealists* in the 1970s merely copy the real with deliberate servility? Of course they did, but their scrupulous perspectives—modern *vedute* of post-industrial cities, service stations and auto bodies with lustrous surfaces—all turned out to be copious focalizations transforming the prosaic conformation of the visible into a hallucinogenic spectacle (where a reflection on chrome as painted by someone like Parrish would rival the effects of the virtuosities of Neapolitan or Dutch still-lifes in the classical age…). In fact, for conventional "realist" art (not to mention politically oriented realist art, in light of its exacerbated penchant, in particular, for the monumentalization of the real), the artistic treatment of reality in the past was hard put to avoid either sublimation, or its most common plastic avatar, the overdone style. Far from past reality being grasped at its own level, far from it merely being "experienced", it ended up on the contrary inserted into the demonstrative, agonistic and almost sport-like logic which is part of the history of representation: it had to be established in terms of difference, remain open to the unheard-of, make reference *in fine* to something other than reality, in a transcendentalist perspective. The example of Warhol, in this respect, is almost inspired caricature, for he embodied a reactivation—extending to previously unattained proportions—of Baudelaire's celebrated verse: *"You gave me your mud and with it I have made gold"*. And reality? The Warholian stance could only manage to incarnate it with an eye to exaltation or dread. Once brought into relation with art, it only acquired meaning insofar as it showed the extent to which the real is the exceptional—in other words, as something not lived as such, which challenges any lived immersion, any experimentation in the strictest sense.

The sort of "out-of sync" phenomenon being referred to, it might be alleged, tends to bear the character of what, at root, is an inevitable accident, consubstantial with the mechanics of creation itself: the ordinary consequence that the artwork imposes on whatever it uses as its capital. After all, a landscape painted by Constable or Monet never claimed to be a landscape *in every respect*. There is always something else, it would so appear, which would provide art with its supreme quality, tearing it in irresistible fashion toward the symbolic: the inexpressible nevertheless expressed, as Paul Klee might have put it; or, to use the terms of a psychoanalyst specializing in artistic questions: the work acting in the gap between the senses as a vector of almost magical potential, without which it would find itself stagnating at the mediocre level of a nondescript object, the exact inverse of an icon. Nevertheless, what is most troubling, and against which there seems to stand an apparently irreducible mental tradition, is the attitude which a considerable number of artists were to adopt in the course of the 1990s, determined as they were to be rid and done with "being out of sync" and to appropriate reality without any concern for embellishing it, to lift it to the rank of an object of exclamation or to divert its use to different ends. The "art of almost nothing", particularly active in France and the United States, was born of this desire for a return to the sources of the unrefined real, a real which they set out to experiment with in all of its forms, without any distancing, including in its most banal variants. And what of the importance of someone like Jean-Jacques Rullier? It consists in starting all over from scratch and considering the world as if nothing at all were known about it; as if the artist, having cast off any demiurgical affectation, having again become the first man—the naïve and original Adamic man—had lost the very desire to represent, the very meaning of *metis*. What, in fact, is a plate? Or a glass? The best way to find out remains to collect glasses and plates and to exhibit them in a gallery for what they are. What is a bridge, a dream, a place of worship? Let's conduct an inquiry, take pictures, do drawings, make lists. Reality, in fact, is alarming, massive, monstrously developed (yes indeed: *many things rather than nothing*); it saps the strength of the man who embraces it, leaving him feeling impotent to grasp it to its full extent, in its true dimensions. Rullier stands for a return to collecting, to that primitive form of world possession. For the Paleolithic to make a comeback in art, it had to take rather than cultivate, to snatch the fruit because the fruit is there, or rather, *already there*. This consciousness of a world envisaged as irrepressible proliferation, as a fragmented unity set at the artist's disposal, was at the same time to nourish the literally Herculean labors of Claude Closky—though what Closky, sibylline Hercules that he is, actually undertook, may to some seem like the most anti-heroic task going. How is the era we are living in to be defined? A work such as *Aujourd'hui* [Today]

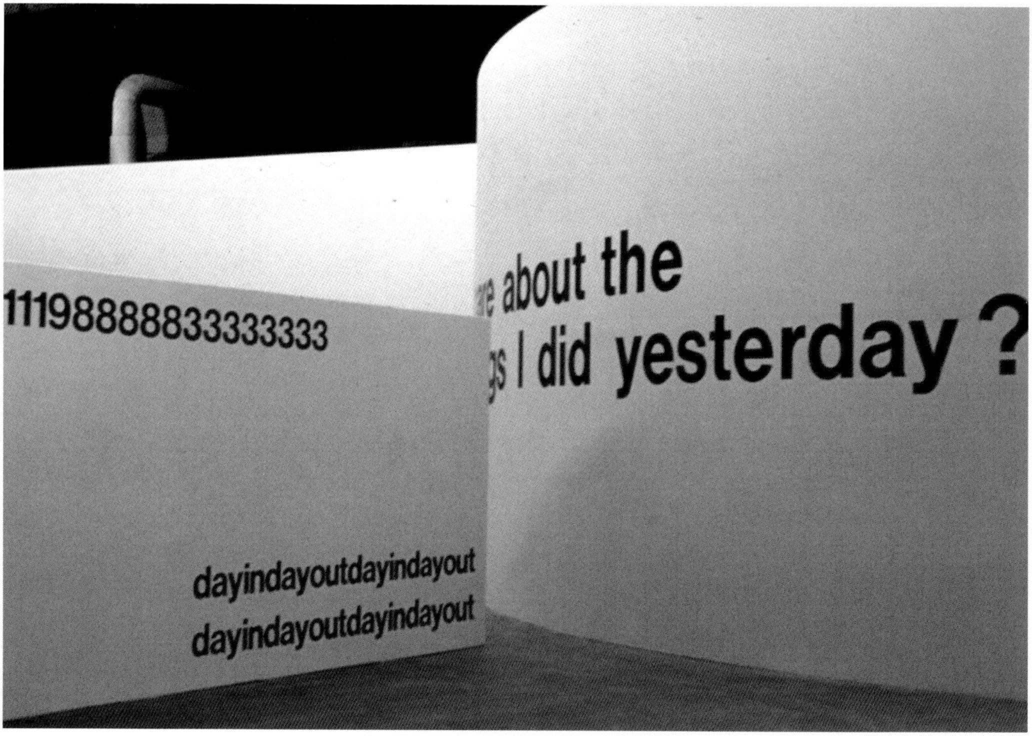

111988888833333333

e about the
gs I did yesterday ?

dayindayoutdayindayout
dayindayoutdayindayout

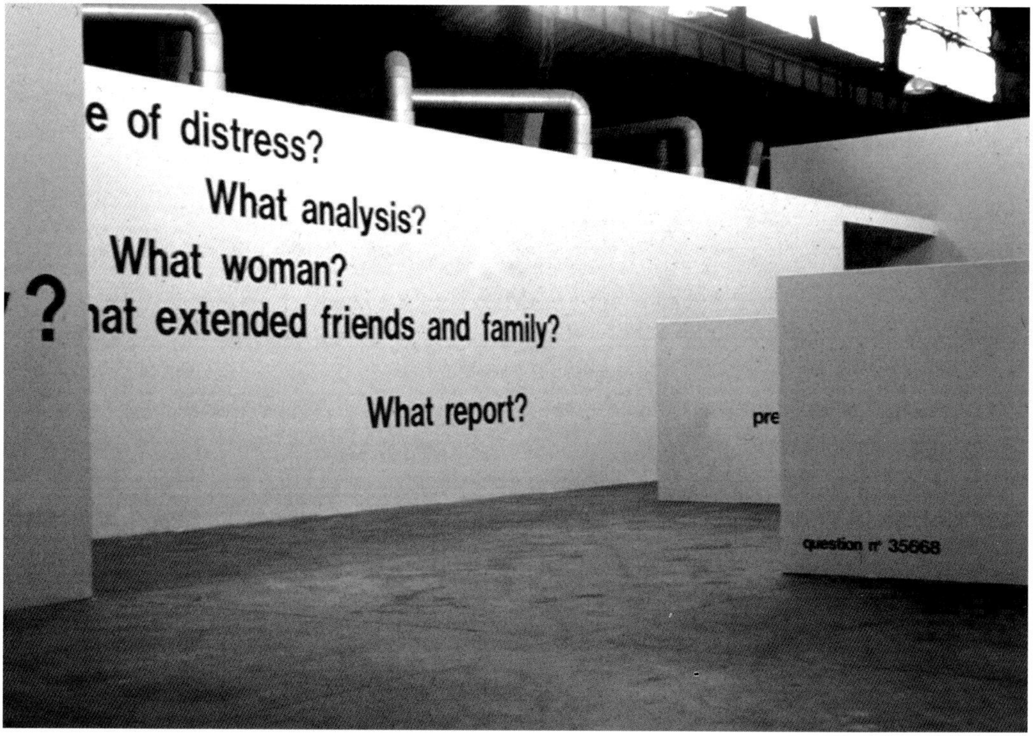

e of distress?
What analysis?
What woman?
? hat extended friends and family?
What report?

pre

question n° 35668

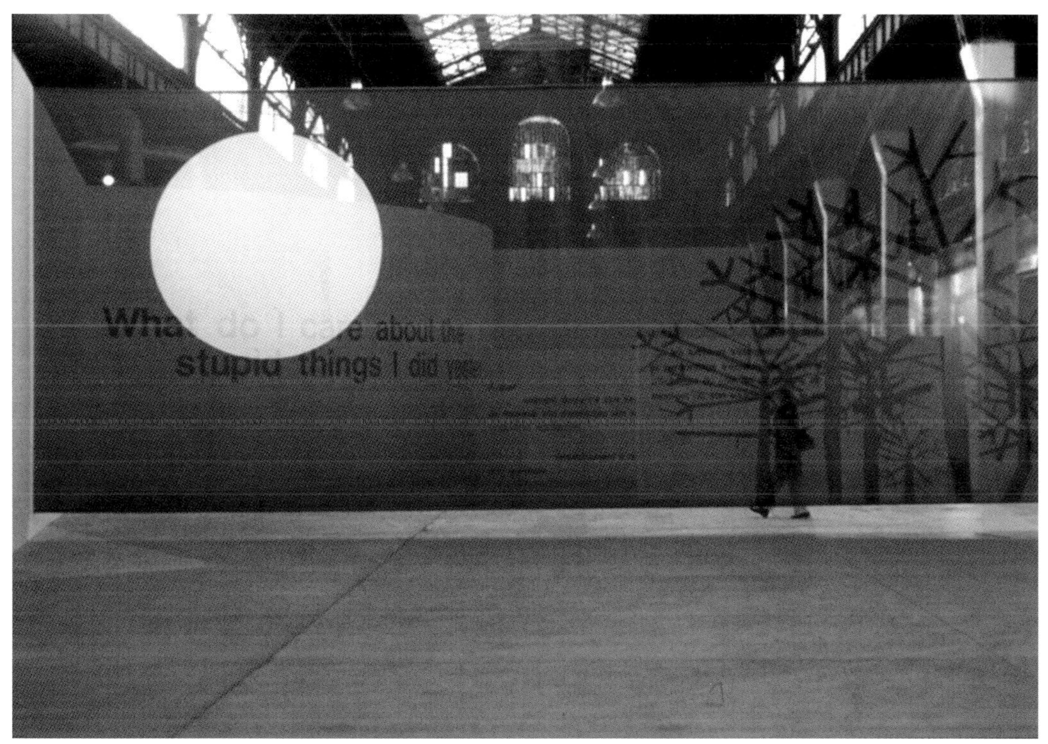

Liam Gillick et Philippe Parreno: *Le procès de Pol Pot*, 1999
Exhibition : Magasin, Centre National d'Art Contemporain de Grenoble (8/11 to 3/01 1999)

thus takes the form of a random collage-style text, made up of dozens of sayings—all outdoing one another in terms of being the last word—that the artist ripped off from the "Society" pages of some magazine or advertising leaflet or other, all of them priding themselves on putting a finger on what "today" is. The result? A constellated rendering of the contemporary real, which is not so far off the mark, and where the truth about our time wells up from the multiplicity of mental clichés Closky has gleaned here and there. A balance sheet of contemporary ways of being? In *Tout ce que je peux être* [Everything I can be], the same Closky accumulated a line-up of adjectives designating the various psychological make-ups available to the late-twentieth-century common man. The enumeration culminates with a convincing psychological portrait in which one is able to read what is henceforth offered by accomplished democratic society in terms of giving unrestricted free rein, at least phantas-matically, to all our penchants. Guy Limone, for his part, stages statistics by means of little figurines or installations: *26% des Français pensent que Dieu est bien le créateur du monde* [26% of the French think that God is indeed the creator of the world]. Statistics? Let's just say that, to date, they provide one of the very best descriptions of the real, indexing incontestable facts that art will do nothing more than pass along, transformed into a procedure for illustrating truths made intangible by the bronze laws of counting and classification. In the end, even life as it is lived will be a muddle of feelings, full and empty moments, in the hold of the everyday where organization is in relentless struggle with disorder, where the man preoccupied with planning his life can suddenly find himself stripped of everything, brusquely self-portrayed with the devalued or extravagant traits of the Nietzschean "being without a plan": all things that Sean Landers' diary entries tackle without compromise, ephemeris leaving nothing to chance or forgetfulness which are merely scribbled hastily on large surfaces called upon to find their way to the exhibition spaces.

Such as it was put together in the course of the 1990s, the notion of "reappropriation" was thus not seized upon by the artists of the "almost nothing" in the name of some conceptual concern or assertive intellectual drive or other, stipulating for instance that the point is now to think of art in this way and no other. If there truly is "reappropriation" (of life but at the very brim of life, of things but in accordance with the primary nature of things), it is in keeping with the sensitive order, in epidermic fashion, because the feeling that something precious, all expectations to the contrary, has been lost: the factual bond, the elementary presence, the sense relationship to primary matter, the naked and deboned "being there". If it is not destined to last (at best it espouses only a moment of the nineties), the "art of almost nothing" nevertheless stands as a timely transitional moment on the tactical front, a militant step of an artistic creation prefigured as an act which sees itself at once as de-intellectualized (conceptual art having ended up by running out of steam) and, insofar as possible, de-idealized. An act initially concerned about living in the world, about "burrowing into its depths", as Gadamer exaltingly put it—but on one express condition: that everything be extracted that can be extracted, with the exception of a metaphysics of form. The discreet but tenacious sign of a return to the real whose productions, of course, would not have inspired any dreams or might even, in their day, have left more than one observer perplexed, though there is no doubt whatsoever that just such an inflection, in its time, had its legitimacy: showing that art could find the road to the elementary, all the elementaries of existence, even those which, on the face of it, seemed the least worthy of interest.

Re-experiencing the link

The forms of "poor" realist art have a disadvantage, moreover quickly diagnosed by their promoters (many of the artists who were part of this tendency soon evolved toward more personal forms[6]): if the bond they reestablish with reality indeed relies on the true experience of lived life, such a link nonetheless remains, once converted into a social value, a *weak* link. This notion of "weakness" (which, symptomatically, was to run through one of the currents of western philosophy for a time, known as "weak thought") is not in itself of a nature to condemn the artistic forms of poor expression. It suggests, on the other hand, that the position of the artist is less social than individualistic, less shared than undivided, less open to difference than condemned to the perpetual return on its solipsistic self. It also validates the possibility that the circle of creation be closed, just as it establishes the principle of an

---

[6] As is testified to by the very development of an aesthetics of the "almost nothing". See, in this regard, the penchant for a realism tempered by the marvelous or the imaginary, consummated by the time lapse between two exhibitions such as *Esthétiques de l'ordinaire* (Mai de la Photo, Reims, 1995, curated by André Rouillé) and *ExtraETordinaire* (Printemps de Cahors, 1999, curated by Christine Macel). On just how this shift came about, see Paul Ardenne, "Un art de la réalité revisitée", in *ExtraETordinaire*, exhib. cat. (Arles: Editions Actes Sud, 1999).

inverted demiurge making the artist into a loner whose isolation creates not unresolvable or sovereign difference but the exact opposite: sameness, similarity, alikeness.

To want to intensify—either through contrast or desire for compensation—the nature of the bond between art and the viewer, to retrace the contour lines of an aesthetic history whose space can be shared in authentic fashion—to get *mobilized*, as much for another as for oneself: these kinds of alternative preoccupations to positions of inward-looking on the artist's part are, assuredly, as old as art itself. We know that modernity, in particular, would direct them toward every imaginable cause, the major result of which was the plastic and topographic widening of its propositions (from the conquest of the free form to that of the free space surrounding the galleries and museums, whether it had to do with the street, untamed nature or communications networks). Hoisted all the way to the postmodern moment, taken back in hand by artists with no inclination either for the solitary experience of the real or abandonment to the sirens of the system, such preoccupations were to enjoy a veritable second lease on life in the nineties. The collapse of the "reality of the self", consecrated by the "art of almost nothing", and the illusion of a public communion which was then complacently conveyed by institutionalized art, would thus correspond to an averred relational fervor, an intense reactivated drive for the sharing of artistic experience. This parallelism is not fortuitous. It is nourished by a will as concerned with rediscovering the Other in the person of the accessible and carnal spectator as it is with being the impulse behind an aesthetic which is truly molded and modulated by reality, demarcated to the greatest possible extent from any vestiges of abandoning the agora as a form of regulating artistic creation by officialdom or the existent general system of art[7].

Though it may take various, highly atomized forms, this movement of a return to the social presents itself in a generic way as an enterprise concerned with realization, right from the inside; it is, moreover, highly attentive to its freedom of movement. It may as well be acknowledged that the physical framework where such a mutation takes place, inclined to create new structures rather than moving into existing ones, appears determinant. Indeed to some extent, it may model and hem the very form of the works which stem from it. Has creation not cut itself some slack since the beginning of the 1990s through self-managed, artist-run spaces where artists themselves present their works, exhibit amongst themselves and organize their own critical promotion? The works resonate with this sort of creation *on the edge* (from the topographical and political edge to the aesthetic edge): aesthetic propositions of limited means, with a high quotient of contention, devoted to rapid consumption and circulation. A sort of duplication in the visual arts' field of what at the same time the fringe movement represented within the world of English-language theater, where an exceptional economy of means is counterbalanced by an exacerbated degree of activism. While this self-managed, self-promotion initiative has not rewritten the laws of the traditional underground, it does however have the particularity of not

---

[7] Studies on these questions, stemming above all from the field of sociology, are numerous and rich. Particularly useful is Raymonde Moulin, *L'artiste, l'institution et le marché* (Paris: Editions Flammarion, 1992). See also Yves Michaud, *L'artiste et les commissaires* (Nîmes: Editions Jacqueline Chambon, 1989), as well as Nathalie Heinich, *Le triple jeu de l'art contemporain* (Paris: Editions de Minuit, 1997), amongst others.

seeking at any price to get into the art system, of remaining marginal, working on the periphery without necessarily petitioning to get the sidelines rezoned as the new center. The very notion of an "artistic periphery", so cherished by the classical avant-garde, is no longer uniformly understood as the point from which the reconquest is to be structured, as if the center alone was of importance. It is to be understood instead as a *topos* devoted to work and "interphalansterian" exchange (small libertarian structure seeks contact with other small libertarian structure)[8]. Understood and experienced in this way, this sort of working on the periphery, or "peripherism", accounts for the aesthetico-social logical specificity of the work being done, as is revealed by an intense concern with *telos* and in which the relationship to reality—experienced as a modulable political space—is emphatically put in the hot seat. The Copenhagen-based, Danish group N 55 opened a shelter for the homeless and invite architects to design a very inexpensive housing. The Austrians from Bricks & Kicks have set up their own structure where they can invite critics and artists to come and promote their original and unassimilated works or theoretical models. Museo Teo in Italy is a structure which is self-run to the extreme: single artists exhibit alone wherever they care to. Various groups of feminist artists in Zurich, taking advantage of the Shedhalle art space's liberalism, set up international meetings and colloquia (*Just Watch*, 1997). Liliane Viala

---

[8] If connection-making is never absent from people's minds, it remains limited. A "semi-alternative" moment *par excellence*, while relations with the institution are, if necessary, being established - but in that case for utilitarian and functionalist purposes, without questioning the autonomy being called for. That is, through financial assistance, the lending of venues, promotional support - all in the perspective of reverse collaboration or instrumentalization, the "institutor" ending up as the "instituted".

and Pierre Dumonthier have initiated a series of private evenings, *On dîne chez qui?* [Whose place are we dining at?], inciting meetings and free speech, and so on. As is scarcely necessary to point out, undertakings such as these are not aiming at any sort of posterity. They have no claim to last, or to see themselves inscribed on the register of the radiant future. As much as focus is placed on the instant, in keeping with the dominant modality of some form of *link art*, there is an equal rejection of the modernist principle of the necessary work. The fundamental criteria? Operability.

This concern with operability, with the confection of works, given weight by a potential for real impact, is anything but minor. The artist working at the end of the twentieth century is fully aware that the socio-political power of his creations is, for the most part, negligible. Traditional realist art, in particular, is not to be imposed with the desired authority. Assailed on its political fringe (not committed enough) as much as for its overly restricted openness (its tutelary duplication principle), it also has the further shortcoming of having a shoddy analytical dimension, of tending toward any number of plastic as well as historical simplifications, and ultimately of being alienated from a conception of reality which is often too close to caricature. And what was classical realist art's ultimate failure? The drive for objectivity (from the pioneers of nineteenth-century realism to the Düsseldorf photography school via the German *Neue Sachlichkeit* of the 1920s) due to an insufficient tension to understand reality for what it is, a tension it was long able to hold under pressure. For objectivity, let us not forget, is nothing but a point of view.

What about making realism succeed? When one gets right down to it, it was the very experience of subjectivity that should have been given priority: the grasping of the world by a body awaiting a revelation (the artist, necessarily *unfinished*), a body which delves into the real as one might into an archeological zone, which envisages its task not as a passive collection but rather as a landscaping initiative to be undertaken with sleeves rolled up. Where objectivity works itself out in the dead image of reality transfixed in movement, subjective experience reveals the exploratory virtues which are in their own way effective in terms of accompaniment and contact. Experience, in this respect, is coextensive and would increase its perimeter and potential only in broadening its field of introspection. In other words, experience's only value is in insistently forcing it own order, reference points and givens in the direction of a reterritorialization of the relationship to reality, making it imperative to pay attention to the context. And the reality? It is doubtless physically finite and mapable: a sum of substances, states and events which can all be objectively tallied. But this "molar" constitution (solid, given, constituted, textualized), as Gilles Deleuze would have said, is just appearance. For one thing because time makes it open-ended. And furthermore because our condition as mortal beings—whose investigative endeavors are in any case limited—makes it into an object in a state of permanent flight, and consequently of precarious configuration. Like humans, contexts are mortal. Like humans, contexts come back with the rhythm of generations. In the opening of coextensiveness, experience tends to capture the reality of the context in proportion to the body being

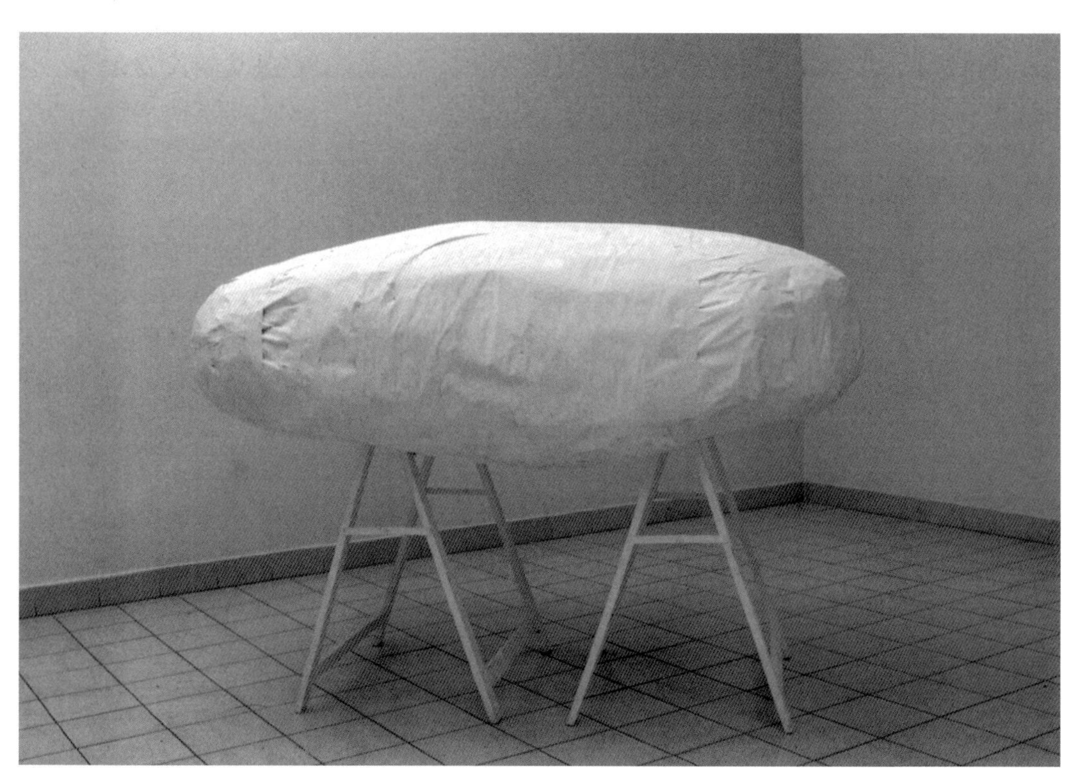

Dan Peterman: *Therm-Guard*, 1993
(Installation)
Collect. FRAC Poitou Charente
Ph: Richard Porteau

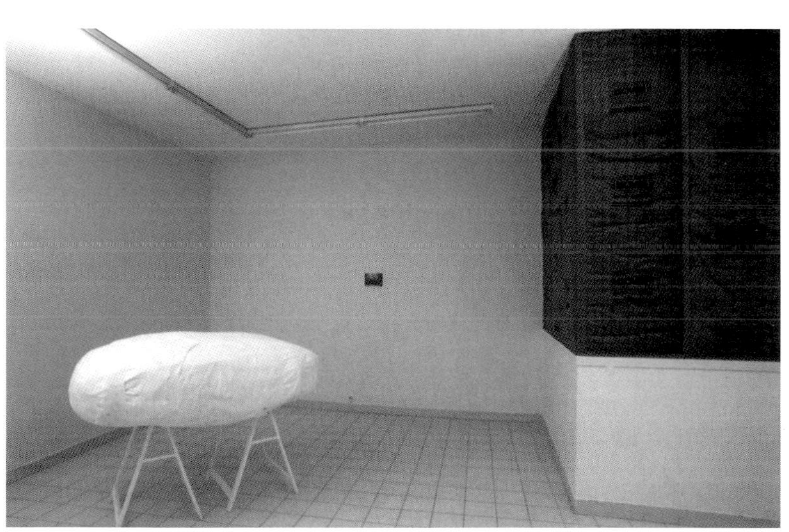

contextualized; it never goes beyond that. To this extent, the physical finiteness of reality is infinite once it has been apprehended in psychological terms.

What about generating operational art, which can be understood as an art coextensive with the real, an art adapted to the context and getting the projection to conform, as geographers say? It is no doubt vain in this respect to claim that art could index the real context *in its entirety*. Chronicle it, sure, in terms of a form of companionship whose way of being will consist in inserting something of the symbolic into the very intensely material order of the contemporary real. And if it fetichistically, fixedly repeats its forms and tendencies, no problem there either. But as for embodying the real (if indeed the purpose of art, regulated as it is by the principle of representation, has ever been about embodiment), that would appear far more difficult to carry off. And even if it were possible, its outcome would be far more uncertain. A successful embodiment will insist that art, though it remains representation, abandon the field of the simulacrum and make its own reality, in a double inscription wherein the work remains an artifact of symbolic content but at the same time hoists itself up to the rank of a factual constituent of reality. The artist's physical input of reality in the strictest sense from that point on appears inevitable, with its two inevitable corollaries being a refusal of the autonomy of the artwork and a rejection of formalism. A refusal of autonomy in that the latter fences the field of creation into a preserve of its separatist and individualist obsessions. A rejection of formalism because the quest for absolute or incomparable form is not soluble *a priori* in an artistic practice that has its sights on the real. All of a sudden, delving into the real involves provoking the paradoxical effect of an act of renunciation: an act imposing the determinant character of the reference. The case in point, the "art of reality" secreted by the very late twentieth century, tardy offshoot of historical realism, is as much as the latter a shackled art. It is out of the question that it cut itself off from reality, consider itself as a prosaic space to be deserted at the earliest convenience. On the contrary, the reference is given and art is set to index everything including itself. An art of reality fatally relinquishes the secret-most part of artistic creation—in other words, that part conjuring up the necessarily stupefying experience where the work is first of all understood not as a putting of world into perspective but as putting one's private self, secret body and deepest being to the test. On the other hand, what it finds there is a non-negligible consolation package: involvement in a social logic, of relational essence.

The debate around "relational aesthetics"

Relational art is doubtless no invention of the nineties. Its roots lie deep in the century: futurism, dada, the Russian avant-garde, without neglecting the sixties and the coronation which they bestowed, on the broadest scale, on formulas for participatory art. We might allow that the nineties, in their own way, calibrated the principle in a less formalist, and less utopian sense. As Nicolas Bourriaud—who was to make "relational aesthetics" one of his battle horses—has shrewdly noted, *"giving form to convivial relations has been a historical constant since the sixties.*

The nineties generation took up the problematic once again, this time unencumbered by the question as to the definition of art, which had been central in the sixties and seventies. The problem is no longer extending the limits of art, but rather about experiencing art's capacities for resistance within the global social field. Out of a single family of practices two radically different problematics can be seen to have arisen: yesterday, the insistence placed upon relations internal to the world of art, within a modernist culture, giving pride of place to the 'new' and calling for subversion through language; today, the stress laid upon external relations in the framework of an eclectic culture where the artwork stands in resistance against the rolling mill of the 'society of spectacle'"[9].

Beyond factual differences that can be accounted for by the change of era, the evolution Bourriaud is getting at actually refers to the supremely cardinal notion of the art sphere—subject, as one might imagine, to variations in scale. Where the artist's manner of working barely changed between the sixties and the end of the twentieth century (the prevalent aesthetics of contact rather than the aesthetics of the contract or observation), it is well and truly the socio-geographical ambition of the latter which is growing. Modern art, of course, was painstaking in creating its sites, *its own* place: in conferring on itself its form, its rules, its manifestoes and museums. The art of the endmost part of the century, on the other hand, has taken over real space again in a perspective of dissolution, infusion and insemination, as if art no longer had its own place, and in

[9] Nicolas Bourriaud, *Esthétique relationnelle* (Dijon: Les Presses du réel, 1998), p. 31.

the end had elected reality to be its natural place of growth. A preeminent moment of generalized importation, of term-for-term exchange: someone like Carsten Höller works along these lines, in the realm of science (on the rules of domesticating animals, for instance, by teaching a finch to whistle original tunes); or someone like Pierre Huyghe in the realm of cinema and the media (remaking famous repertory films, setting up casting sessions); someone like Rirkrit Tiravanija in the domain of cultural or culinary coordination (providing musical instruments to the public or organizing meals). Philippe Parreno and Liam Gillick mandate themselves to lay the groundwork for a reflection of international scope, with the mediation of sponsors, on the botched trial of a dictator (*Le Procès de Pol Pot*, 1998). There is also talk of "remixing", an instrumental form of the remake, disconnected from the original, of recycling and aesthetic redistribution. And many works are no longer even presented to the spectator except in the transitory form of work sites (Stéphane Calais, Jason Rhoades…) or sense-oriented interfaces with a distractive vocation (the moves of the techno DJ, in the clutches of bodily trance).

And reality in that case? Simply by virtue of being lived through, being lived in, it finds itself experimentally applied to a radical usage of synaesthesia where what is given and what takes place "in truth" and "for real" is swiftly incorporated into the bloodstream of art in transfusional or viral fashion. A time of "correspondences" where nature is less a place that emits the sort of jumbled words that Baudelaire discerned in it, than a milieu symmetrical with the new aesthetic *maniera*, where the mutual availability of art and the real sees the traditional questions so dear to analytical philosophy get thrown head over heels—and above all such questions as: "What is art?" Or, following Goodman: "When is art?" In this regard, art is, if needs be, the real itself, unconcerned about any obligatory symbolization (Raymond Hains was able to say with regard to his works that they existed in the natural state, in a real space, but that prior to his extracting them from it, no one seems to have noticed or have taken any pains to see them). Art, all the time, non-stop, in an uninterrupted and unlocalized flow. A fusion between art and the real, which, as it is easy to imagine, will spark the worst criticism, the de-hierarchization it consecrates extending in this case further than the habitual "de-definitions" (Rosenberg) which had hitherto affected the realm of art. For this time round, the art of reality truly seems to merge with the reality of art, while the circulation between the two polarities seems to have been rendered *null and void*, the effect of a reciprocal contribution. But let's not be fooled: what some people will assess, in the bemoaning mode, to be the "end of art" (but its final end, they will argue, not the mime of a Lazarean agony where resurrection lies watching in the wings, awaiting a new saving *novum*), is in fact nothing other than one of the forms of its plenary realization.

Art and politics at the hour of the promise's end

Talk about reality, make reality talk, sure. But what are we talking *about*? And what, very exactly, is "reality"? Does the singular form even make any sense? Because reality, at least on the postmodern calendar, is above all *realities*. The current mood is no longer for mental schematizations, square definitions, the sole dimension of it principal property, but rather for clashing together, dismantling, complex linking, decrystallization. Gilles Deleuze et Félix Guattari, published *A Thousand Plateaus* in 1981[10]. The book was to be a beacon whose light was like that of a crystal, with multidirectional beams. It put forth a powerful image, rendering it in a way that was as hallucinatory as it was lucid, of a polydimensional real in a state of global facetting, made up of rhizomes and fragmentation, reticulated all over, infinitely sectioned by private initiatives, liberated drives and incessantly reconfigured network structures. A thousand layers of reality—indeed, reality is a thousand layers—whereas the western individual finds himself "segmented from all sides", his only settlement being the ever more alarming profusion of contexts, born of the segmentarization of desires and actions. What from now on has been rendered highly improbable is the definition as much of a stationary "situation" (the Sartrian moment has passed) as of a single existential or political objective. As Mikka Hannula writes, *"in each given context there are always specific values and criteria, and different versions in terms of the objectives of the truth."* What then is to be said of a world in which the multiplicity of contexts is equaled only by that of multiple desires, projected as if they were free into a state of circulation[11]?

Experimenting, by means of art, with a relational adventure is, in and of itself, to enter the terrain of politics. One may as

[10] Gilles Deleuze and Félix Guattari, *A Thousand Plateaus: capitalism and schizophrenia*, translated by Brian Massumi (Minneapolis: University of Minnesota Press, 1987).
[11] Mika Hannula, "Please, No More Guitar Heroes ", in *Interpreting Contemporary Art*, (Helsinki: Ateneum Publications, 1998), p. 95.

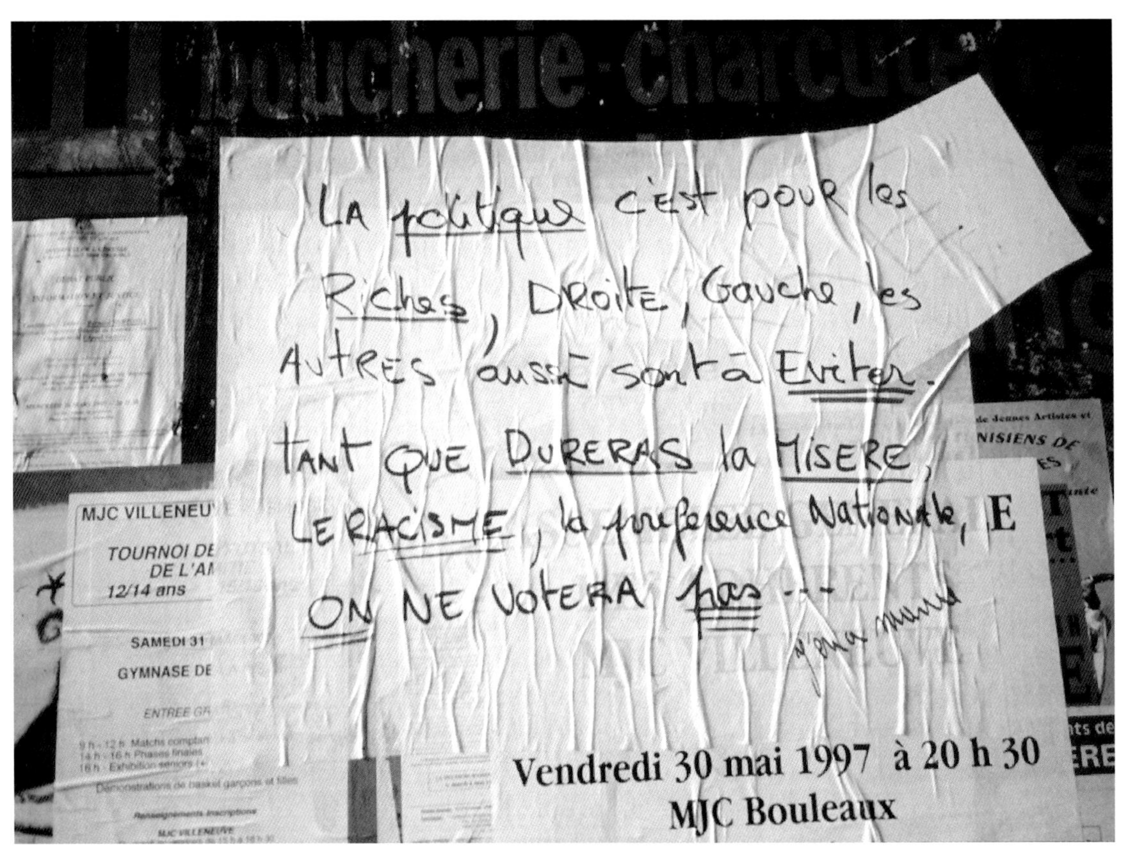

Nick Gee: n° 92 séries *Perte de temps?* (20 05 97 - 10h05)

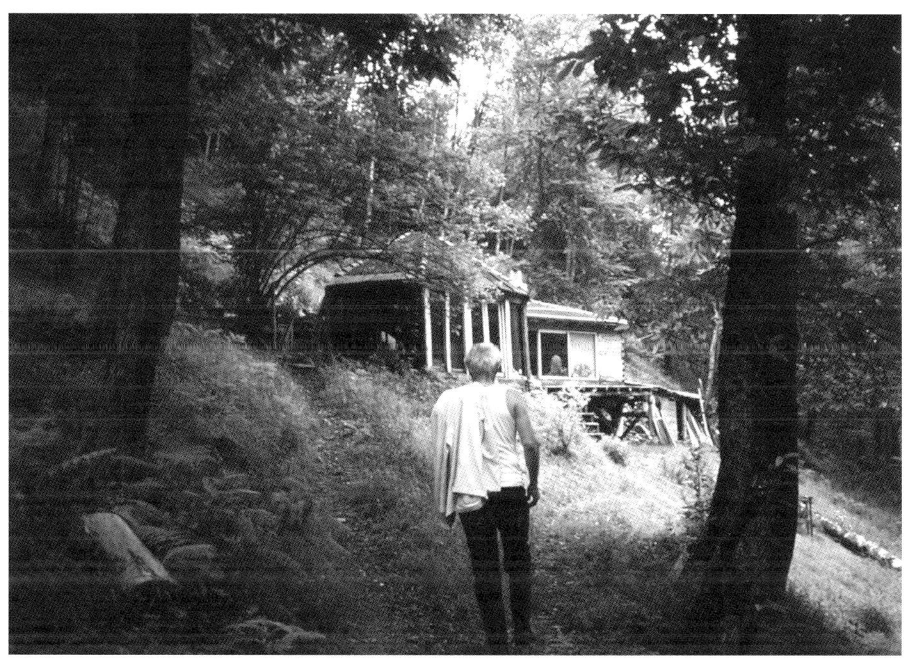

Nick Gee: n° 135 séries *Qu'oserais-je dire….*(13 07 97 - 16h00)

well, by way of a shortcut, just talk about experimenting with politics itself, though an artist's means differ from those of a traditional politician. There is nothing easy about it, if one is prepared to follow Jacques Rancière and admit that "politics" in the modern sense of the term, regulated by the promise principle has had its day: *"the end of politics, the rumor of which is running all the streets, is gladly described as the end of a certain time, itself marked by a certain wear of time, the wear of the promise"*[12]. In terms of understanding, nothing further will be promised because the mood of the day has turned from productive utopia to management and accountable organizational logic. Not that utopia is dead; it has become "realistic utopia", rump utopia: a proposal for proper management, a minimal harmony at best, the great dreams having been put away in the attic of nineteenth-century ideological curios. An art organized by the notions of "sync" and "adaptation", mentioned above, in such a context, would thus be unable to promise anything without being immediately out of step, grandiloquent, even ridiculous. That the extreme end of the twentieth century sound the death knell for the hitherto admitted forms of committed art is, in this respect, not surprising. What is to be said of someone like Joseph Beuys' shaman-like invocations, dedicated to the redemptive restoration of the collective word, now that the words are only waiting to be broken down, scattered about the real like crumbs? The denunciations of barbarity by artists like Hans Haacke and Jochen Gerz are so didactic, so demonstrative in their form, that they refer back to a

---

[12] Jacques Rancière, "La fin de la politique ou l'utopie réaliste" [1988], in *Aux bords du politique* (Paris: La Fabrique- Éditions, 1998), p. 18.

time based on frontal conceptual oppositions. Not that the political commitment of the artist has become irreversibly obsolete, but it must evolve.

Two major axes structure political aesthetics as the twentieth century draws to a close. One is oriented toward factual operativeness: Antoni Muntadas, with the *File Room* (1995), put artistic creation into the service of the struggle against censorship; Krysztof Wodiczko, with his public art installation (*Homeless Vehicle*, a survival vehicle intended for the homeless, in 1988, *Alien Staff*, a work for immigrants, in 1992…), produces an art of denunciation aiming at the reduction of collective tension. What such propositions have going for them is their immediateness, their capacity to flush out tension wherever it is, their deep-seated anti-ideality. Their shortcoming, on the other hand, stems from the vagueness of their exact intentions, which might come together with those of NGOs (in terms of fighting censorship, Amnesty International is more effective than anyone else…) or blend in with the economy of the spectacular governing every form of intervention in the collective milieu: the best intentions of exploiting the public sphere are apt to go awry. A second tendency, which was to experience major expansion, is particularly fond of installations that are almost mute in terms of the senses: public propositions are made (posters, electronic banners, street interventions…) but without the precise meaning being given. These formulas which leave interpretation, if not free, then at any rate open, are fed by an anti-authoritarian generic will. No directive discourse. The important thing, at root, is that the intervention, as Gordon Matta-Clark suggested in his day, must be "capable of turning structure into a communicative act", this communication initiating a rise in consciousness which the spectator will either develop or not, and of greater importance in such a case than the meaning of what is actually communicated. That is essentially, for the advocates of the second way, the chosen manner for getting around the pitfall of the spectacular and the directiveness which is invariably lying in wait for the procedures of artistic intervention. Just as classical committed art, yielding sooner or later to sloganeering, and in so doing making the denunciation into an injunction, always gives way to the declaration of authority—and, consequently, turns out to be no better than the authority it is fighting against—an interventionist art which allows only the spectacle itself to be seen will ultimately constitute a form of visual authoritarianism, referring more to a grammar of order than to a true challenge of established values. It is patent that many "old-style" formulas for artistic intervention, in this respect, have some difficulty in getting beyond the *fairground* stage. Such formulas end up feeding, most often despite themselves (such blindness with regard to their own purposes is hard to forgive), the economy of organized activity which the western world literally reveres—a form of organized activity the west pays lip service to challenging even while embodying one of the least expected and hence most exciting forms of it there is *a priori*.

Actually, a common means of artistic intervention in the public sphere at the end of the twentieth century consists not in adding to the already existent, but on the contrary, in *subtracting* from it. Such, once again, is the lesson drawn from the methods of Matta-Clark, explicitly those linked to the principle of "anarchitecture" which the artist began developing in New York from 1974 on. For the "anarchitect", architecture, as the material doublet of an era's cultural reality, provides an instructive and revealing case. From a building's envelope, the "shell" representing the equivalent of the skin for the body, we know that it is most often concealing the organs instead of bringing out their functionality to the light of day: a concealment orchestrating as much the necessity of grandeur (something has to be seen, of spectacular nature if possible) as the need for withdrawal (the hidden as the ignoble or problematic antithesis of the exhibited part). Driven by a concern for critical inventory, the anarchitect thus engages in *excavation*, in the exhibition of structures ordinarily lifted out of the frame of organized vision. From a practical point of view—following that of Matta-Clark himself—his work would consist of subtracting and sectioning, in revealing the "negative space" which forms the building's structural underpinnings. In his 1972 work *Wallpapers*, Gordon Matta-Clark exhibited the wall surfaces of a house in the throws of being demolished, whose walls had all been wallpapered: it was an act of laying bare the intimacy habitually refused to collective vision and the specific decorative codes governing it. In *Splitting*, a performance done in 1974, a house at 332 Humphrey Street, in Englewood, New Jersey, was divided by a vertical line, and half of it was shifted by five degrees, such that a breach was opened providing a view both of the interior and, as in an autopsy, of the rules governing the architectural harmony. The aesthetics implicit in anarchitecture sculpt social space by pointing out how we organize our own lives within it. It implicitly shows the conditioning inherent in our way of living and our hierarchical and norm-based representations of both the public and private spheres, based upon stark oppositions: inside—outside, intimacy—sociality, exhibition—concealment, visible—invisible, open—closed, accessible—inaccessible, and so on. His work staged with great clarity our impenitent appetence for encoding—an irrefutable sign of alienation.

Subtracting, it may as well be pointed out, has over the course of the past quarter century been one of the preferred means of action for "interventionist" artists. Dan Graham, installing his two-way mirrors here and there throughout the public sphere, forces the spectator to question his own social image, his way of being, of reacting in front of other people. Jenny Holzer's *Truisms*, pouring out messages on electronic billboards, whose content is at once familiar and inquisitive ("To die for love is beautiful but it's stupid"), summon meaning only to snatch it away immediately. The same appetance, in various forms, can be found in the work of Barbara Kruger, Daniel Buren, or in some of Peter Downsborough's or François Morellet's public artworks: playing publicly with a private form, offering forms but not meaning, providing a sensitivity that its structure materializes but which remains immaterial in terms of its meaning. It is a logic of "inorganic" intrusion: an elegant response to heavy, cumbersome installations, often sinisterly void of any content and specificity, typical of traditional urban art, dependent on commission, which actually aestheticize the control of whoever is doing the commissioning over the artist being commissioned.

Micropolitics

Some will feel that the "political" artist, whose identikit portrait we have just sketched out, has no personal vision, and no historical project. Like the idle figure, once again, of the "man without a plan", he will be called a mere wisp of flesh floating in the maelstrom of spineless reality which it is no longer worth analyzing or challenging. Let us not let them down. This artist, indeed, stands as if in the background, making his background position into a sanctuary. He has given up, for the most part, on direct, unmediated action. He no longer has the modern concern of the sixties performer to eliminate any distance between himself and the spectator. This attitude, in spite of appearances, is not nihilistic. It results rather from prudence. For each position occupied with excessive firmness becomes, more or less, a commonplace: a site of an increasing focus, soon visited to excess, saturated, where the best initial formulas can quickly turn into caricature. If by nature art is the occasion for a social bond, there is nothing to indicate that the occasion can do the job every time and that the thread woven with the spectator must invariably conform to the skein of generalized exchange developed at the outset. Once again, we are confronted with the effects of "getting out of sync", or of conditioned responses that end up by wearing out the most noble of intentions. Not to mention the frequent naiveté presiding over artistic endeavors concerned with negating the distance between the work and the spectator, in particular those using the collective space of the street, a milieu of being together and of the tribal mix, supposed to be conducive to facilitating inevitable contact. In fact, to believe that shrinking the physical space between the work and the spectator would be able to bring the two together, as if the organization of *placement* alone could bring about a veritable exchange, is like believing that integral promiscuity, on the political and social level, is a uniting factor and the cement of the perfect society (regrettably, though, we know that it is just the opposite which prevails: there is no real society without social differentiation, without conflict, without violence, without frustration, whereas the "text" structuring the power, as Pierre Legendre would say, the law itself, sole guarantee of bearable conditions for living together, indeed acts as a damper upon my desire for the Other).

To a large extent, it is as an art of subtracted meaning, that, with the end of the twentieth century, art with political content is being increasingly constituted. Not, in fact, that there is no meaning to it. *Something at least remains: our impenitent will to confer a meaning upon everything, but in this case highlighted in the lack of meaning itself.* As a coherent practitioner of what he evocatively refers to as *Actions peu* [Barely actions], Boris Achour walks around Paris' Place Vendôme, past the jewelers' shop windows, with the following Sibylline logo blazoned onto his tee-shirt: "Les femmes riches sont belles" [Rich women are beautiful]. The same artist, moving on to Paris' Luxembourg Gardens, becomes the "Liner-Upper of Pigeons" by spreading wheat and corn seeds on the ground in long, straight lines. The *"action peu"*, in defiance of all heroism, not only fights for the vanity of high artistic discourse, it also claims, in the name of the artist, a portion of freedom which had previously always been stingily meted out, and the right to remain indifferent to the prevailing artistic code without even caring to amend it, subvert it or make fun of it. The spectator, one way or the other, will end up making what he likes out of it. As for Raphaël Boccanfuso, he does highly intriguing *Actions stationnaires* [Stationary actions], using a process repeated over and over again: he parks his Citroën BX in front of various contemporary art exhibition spaces, having previously decorated the vehicle with a various slogans next to the recurrent theme, *Les priorités de R. B.*[R.B.'s priorites]: *"Tenir le haut du pavé"* [Head the field], *"Etre n° 1"* [Be number1], *"Etre bien vu"* [Be well seen], *"Entrer en contact"* [Get into contact], and so on. What is Boccanfuso driving at? Of his own will to find a place in the field of art? An obsession with public recognition? Logics of seduction at work in the artistic milieu, or, more broadly, on the scale of the entire society[13]? Any hypothesis one might care to put forth, in this case, is acceptable. Let it be noted that as far as both Achour and Boccanfuso are concerned, we see the same regard for *action*— a term that is indexed with aesthetic logic in the very title of the works proposed to the spectator by both artists. For it should be recalled through comparison, if only to measure the road taken, what "action" meant to the Viennese, or even "event" to George Brecht, thirty years before: a radical, carefully aimed gesture, saturated with subversion, the depository of an incontestable critical dimension which now seems to be deliberately lacking (criticism's first concern is the definition of

[13] See, in particular, *Cet été là... Exposition de variétés*, exhib. cat. (Sète: Centre régional d'art contemporain du Languedoc-Roussillon, July-October 1998), p. 60, which includes reproductions of *Actions stationnaires*.

a loved or hated object), the precise object that is being questioned here not having been determined strictly speaking.

Some will doubtless describe these aesthetic formulas, exceptional above all for their sought-after and accepted mediocrity, as the art of an era characterized by the Lyotardian end of the "great narratives". The art of a time where politics escapes those who set the rules as much as it does those supposed to submit to them; where the factual indecision of the collective contract is expressed by an equivalent level of indecision in the plastic propositions whose objective it is to address "social issues". An art of intermittent or partial contact, conditional upon a preserved form of freedom (freedom of judgment, action and belief), whereas the artist refrains from abandonment either entirely to himself or entirely to the other. An art, to sum up and synthesize, which has to do with *micropolitics*. Instead of speaking on the rostrum, artists speak in their neighborhoods: in Tania Mouraud's *City Performances*, beginning in 1978, postered views of the third world are distributed in some corner of the immense western city, without any further commentary. There is no more speaking in place of other people, but as the artist takes up the listening position, they are given the opportunity to speak if need be: Sylvie Blocher's videotaped interviews are free proposals to speech, offered to anonymous candidates, without any restrictions whatsoever. If there is no more changing the world, at least there is observation, at least there is questioning, including on the issue of how best to make the uninhabitable in western societies inhabitable: Dan Peterman, through works that are at once symbolic and functional, reflects on the problem of pollution and the objective possibilities to reduce the damage; Nick Gee takes the pretext of a local strike in a southern French town, to create an installation bringing together political reflection, social solidarity and the question as to the aesthetic treatment of the class struggle (*Qu'oserais-je dire?* [What do I dare say?], 1997). "Micropolitics", hemmed in by nothing, is also concerned with production, the organization of material reality, the sometimes contradictory uses of productivism, which it infinitely mirrors or replays in a distanced mode, inviting the viewer to overturn prejudices and acquired points of view. Simon Sterling, in 1997, produced a truly astonishing work: the young Scottish artist built a Marin-brand bicycle using a Charles Eames aluminum chair, and *vice versa*. Uri Tzaig's artistic work, classified under the emblem of "re-experience", develops surprising disruptions whose aim consists in requalifying certain social usages, notably those in the world of sports: a second ball is inserted into the coded economy of a football match, filmed, moreover, as if the rules of the game were unknown to the cameraman[14]. With *A.C. Forniture sud vs Cesena 12 to 47 1991 Fussball*, a benchmark work, Maurizio Cattelan "staged" the reality of ordinary hatred and social delinquency in a playful and thoroughly disarming manner: the artist had a team he had put together play in the regional circuit of the Italian Calcio—a team made up of immigrant Senegalese players whose jerseys bore the nazi slogan *"Rauss!"*

---

[14] Uri Tzaig, *Re-experience*, catalogue published for Manifesta 1, Rotterdam (Tel Aviv: The Israeli Society for Culture and Art, 1996).

Accepting the heterogeneity of a whole

"Micropolitical" art, unadorned and unafflicted, is an instance of what it confirms at the same time: that the scope of "reality art" as envisaged by the very end of the twentieth century, whether of the "micropolitical" order or not, is limited. By design, let us point out. Its claim is first and foremost the local essence, not the range of the universal. The artist of reality? His position, in keeping with this placement, is that of humility. It will be admitted that the real, having become the focal point of his work, also provides its *tempo*. This relinquishment of the real—and let us stress this point—which will be lived through without suffering. One last time, Baudelaire's entreaties are to be repeated—this time so they may be forgotten. For Baudelaire, the artist giving himself over to reality, shackled hand and foot, has truly ceased to *respect* art: *"From one day to the next"*, writes the author of the *Flowers of Evil* along these very lines, *"art loses respect for itself, grovels before external reality, and the painter becomes ever more inclined to paint not what he dreams, but what he sees"*[15]. Or take Delacroix' equally rancorous comment: *"Hey, confounded realist, are you by any chance trying to produce an illusion such that I might figure I was actually a witness to the spectacle you are claiming to offer me?"*[16]. Delacroix, whose anti-realist remarks continue in this vein, setting the horizon, beyond romantic art, of a phantasmatics of artistic creation which accepts the artist only insofar as he abandons himself to the dream of a complacent transcendence

[15] Charles Baudelaire, *Curiosités esthétiques - Salon de 1859* (Paris: Éditions Bordas, 1990), p. 319.
[16] Quoted by Marcel Zahar, *Courbet* (Genève: Editions Pierre Caillet, 1952), p. 60.

and of an insolvent career as the messenger boy of the Absolute: *"It is the cruel reality of objects from which I flee when I take refuge in the sphere of the creations of Art"*. Anathema such as these are no longer in season. "Reality art", ultimately—and whatever the costs may be in terms of worldly respectability—acknowledges its congenital incompatibility with the demiurgic powers. An acceptation which forces the course of a western culture keen on productions considered to be devoted to a form of symbolic excellence which it would otherwise be their historical mission to perpetuate[17]. An acceptation which holds that the important thing, henceforth, is not so much to create (in the sense of *Schöpfung*—creation as something which adds) as to codify the world such as it is, in the state we have put it in. At the cost, it goes without saying, of a contact that dissipates you, reduces you still further, throws you onto the ropes, headlong into a cadenced reality (the world as that which never wants to end and has not stopped childbearing), profuse with works which will never be but fragments of a whole which itself is fragmented. As Daniel Buren has pointed out, in a timely formula: *"Of course I don't think that the autonomy of the work ever exists.... The isolation of the work is over and done with, we have to accept the heterogeneity of a whole."*[18]

[17] On these points, see Serge Bismuth, *Rire des maîtres de l'art moderne*, Doctoral thesis (Université de Paris I, 1995), above all chapter III, "Les structures de la fin ", which includes a very keen analysis of the *effet de réel.*
[18] Daniel Buren, in *À force de descendre dans la rue, l'art peut-il enfin y monter ?* (Paris: Editions Sens & Tonka, 1998), pp. 73-74.

next page

Sylvie Blocher: *Living Pictures/Gens de Calais*, 1997
video installation, 35 mn, sceen 275x400cm

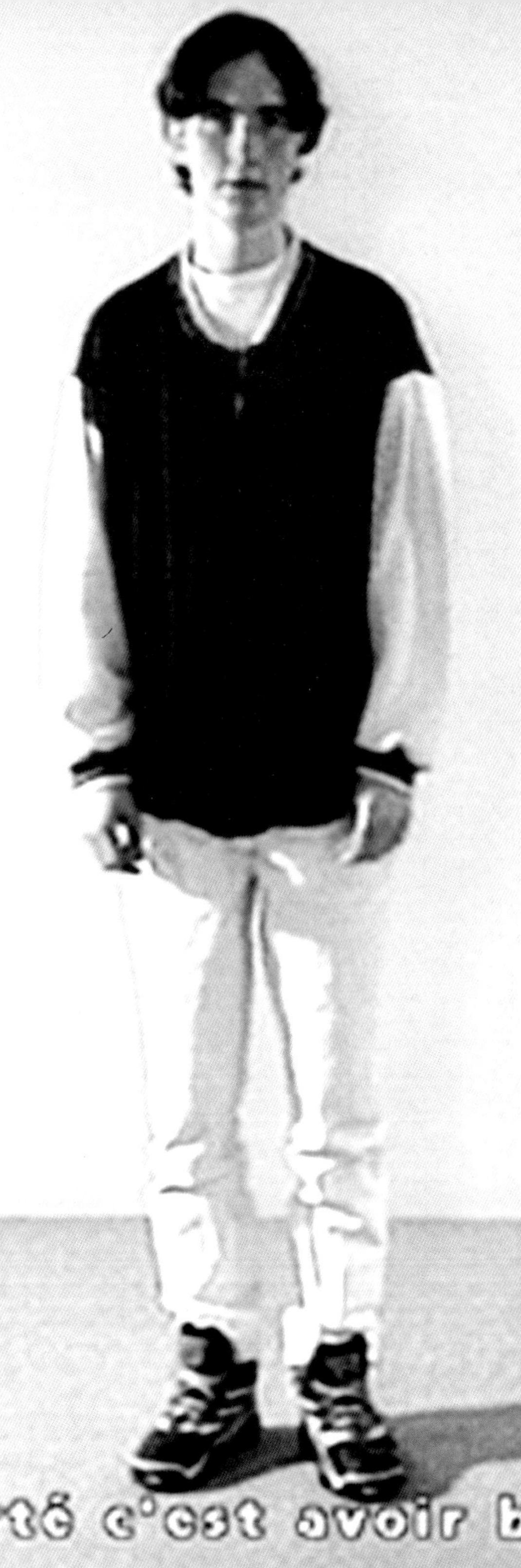

la fierté c'est avoir beaucoup

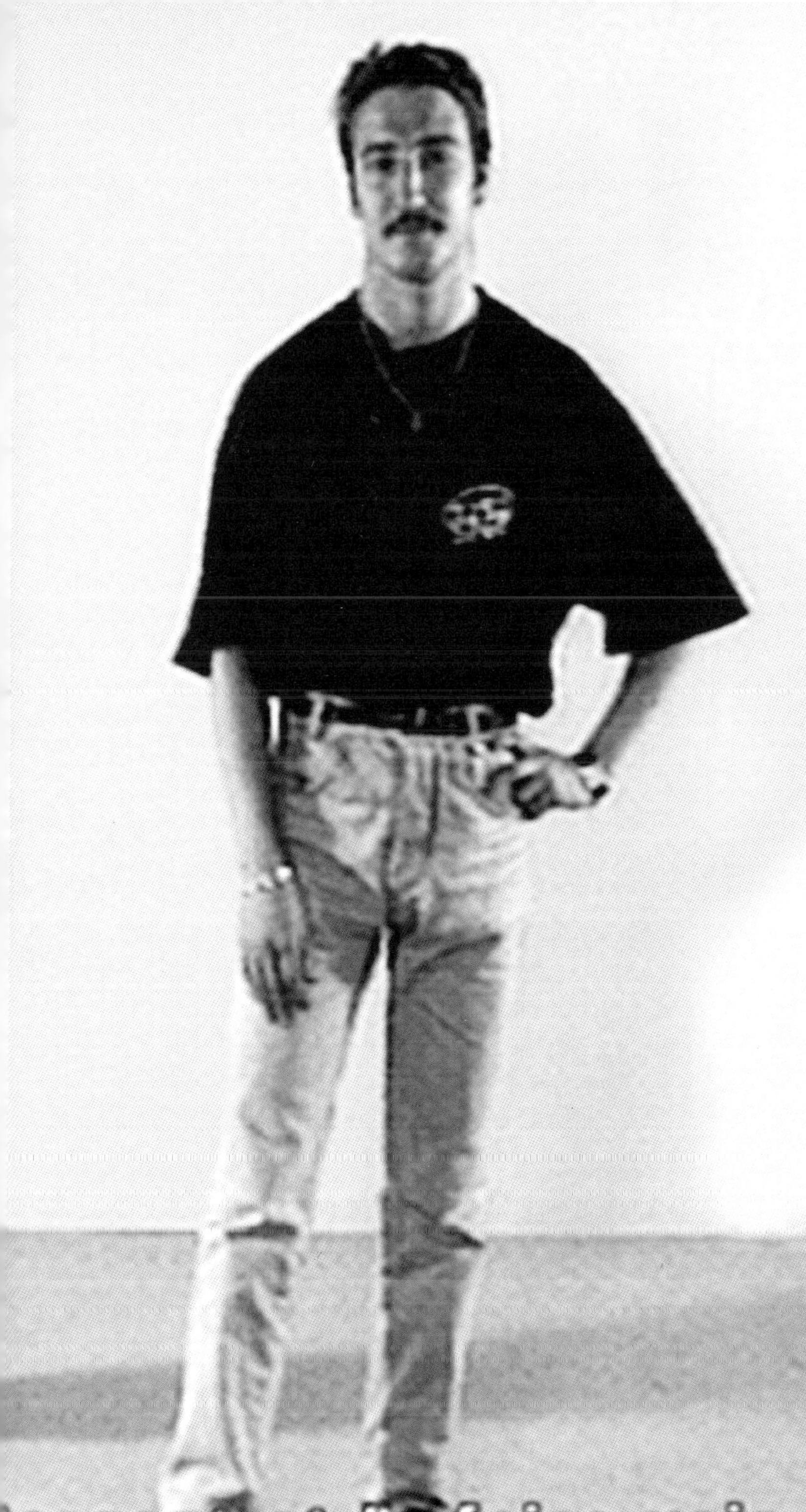

l'argent et le faire voir

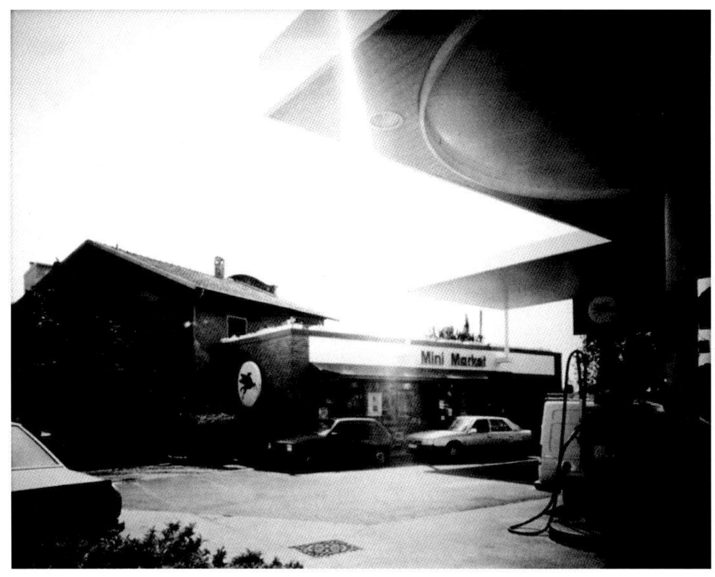

Bruno Serralongue: *n°25, mardi 26 avril 1994*
cibachrome and sérigraphy, 87 x 105 cm
courtesy Air de Paris

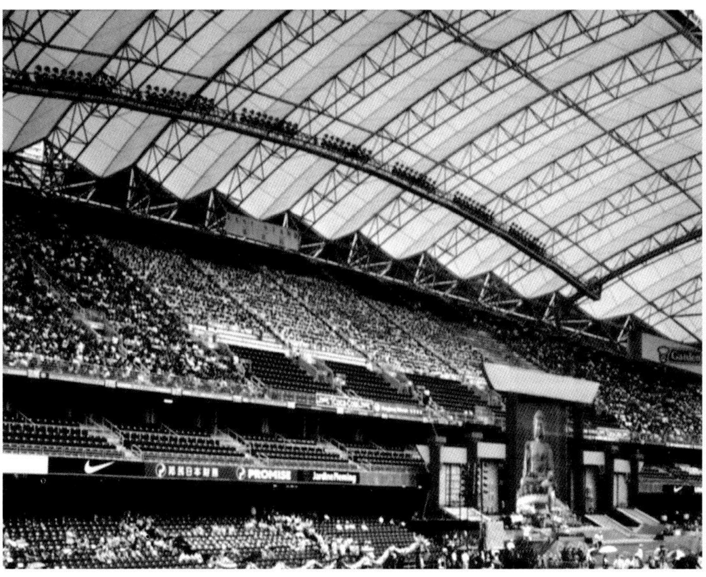

Bruno Serralongue:
Buddhist Gathering for Celebration of Unification, Hong Kong, 01 07 97, 1997
cibachrome, 124 x 157cm
(série *Handover*)
courtesy Air de Paris

Information:
Inquiries into the Real and the Self-media

Can art, in the age of the information society, stand aside from the large-scale fabrication of representations of the real? Are artists, with the means at their disposal, equipped to advance forms of reality other than those put forward by the information and entertainment industries? The complex phenomenon of economic globalization is marked not only by the virtualization of the workplace and by powerful surges of goods and capital around the globe, but also by a revolution in the information industry. In this context, the mass media have established themselves as the great stagers of reality. The continuous flood of visual, acoustic and written information produced and diffused each day by the mass media tends to hide the real lack of representation of social reality; yet these same media are the effective agents of that very reality.

Given the uniformity of the image system and the all-powerful advance of a simplifying message, can artistic activity allow itself to relinquish its function of representation? Can today's artists still respond in any way to the abstraction produced by powerful financial interests and the smoke screens set up by commodity fetishism? It is not a question of going to battle against media representations; for the economy's control over the everyday visual environment is so tight that the battle is already lost. Rather, artistic activity is faced with the requirement to confront the regimes of visibility of this new image paradigm, and to try to dismantle its coding systems. It is clear that, recently, too much importance has been granted to an art based on withdrawal into the sphere of the private. Yet artists still cannot avoid the public sphere.

In every one of its manifestations, from the most global to the most local, the real is, today more than ever, a fascinating area for exploration. While art history has been preoccupied with the question of realism since the invention of the technological image during the second industrial revolution, it has never before been more tuned in to the real itself. Since the end of the 1960s (post-Pop), after a steady stream of movements that took refuge in formalism despite their claim that they were dealing with life, there has been a real desire to place artistic production within the historical context from which it emerged. Notwithstanding certain contradictions, in the early 1970s some conceptual artists like Dan Graham, Hans Haacke and David Lamelas laid the groundwork for an art that would be in tune with society and history.

In the next generation, which was shaped by Conceptual Art, a few rare artists (with Allan Sekula and Martha Rosler in the lead) established a type of critical approach to the real. Their creation of a crisis among documentary modes of representation, which showed the "inadequacy"–to use Martha Rosler's term–of all media in the face of the real, undoubtedly raised the possibility of multiple investigative procedures in the minds of artists of the 1990s.

Another type of information

The inquiry into the real assumes numerous shapes. Going beyond sociological or journalistic models, it attempts to propose another type of information about the real. In this case, the "forming" involved in each piece of information does not mean the use of stylistic effects but seeks, above and beyond any personal touch, to break free of existing codes and formats of representation. The information produced by the artist is not that "password" described by Deleuze.[1]

In the work of the artists covered in this essay we find no naive beliefs in the power of the image, and no fantasies about the purity of this or that medium. Quite to the contrary, it shows that it is free to pick up, successively or simultaneously, any number of tools (for a medium can be nothing other than a tool) in order to interrogate the real.

It should be understood by now that the subject of this essay is not technology in itself, but the effects produced by the spread of the informational model, from public space to the specialized sphere of artistic activity. The artists that matter to

---

[1] Gilles Deleuze, "Qu'est-ce que l'acte de création?" *Trafic*, no. 27, Paris (Fall 1998), pp. 133-142.

me do not go about making icons of the fetish objects produced by industry, nor do they adopt the information processing lexicon as their model out of some naive optimism in the technical possibilities of multimedia. Must we be reminded that at each appearance of a new technique we see the same opposition between eulogists of progress and obtuse conservatives? Both camps reiterate the same arguments with which their ancestors met the invention of photography, the telegraph, cinematography, the telephone and television, although the situation is probably more farcical in the world of art than in that of civil society. Each new medium brings along with it a succession of unreasonable myths based on blind faith in–or fear of–the idea of progress. I need only mention two misconceptions nourished by the currency of such myths.

The dematerialization of information through electronics, the democratization of the worldwide web and the extension of the Derridean concept of deconstruction have led some people today to conceive of the work world as a virtual environment. However, the products of borderless industrial activity are not transported from continent to continent by e-mail or plane but, as Allan Sekula has pointed out,[2] by ship, by that maritime world that has been forgotten.

Given the possibilities offered by digital recording in combination with image retouching software, it has been said that we are now entering an era of falsity in photography. To say this is to forget that retouching has always been a part of photography and that an early photographer like Gustave

---

[2] See Allan Sekula, *Fish Story* (Düsseldorf: Richter Verlag, 1995).

Legray used several negatives to construct his images. This new myth of a falsity of the image is as naive and ignorant of the technical and semantic realities of the medium as the myth it replaced. I am referring, of course, to the equally radical myth of "truth in photography."

This said, there is a real need to question the possibility (or impossibility) of representation, and to do so by going far beyond just the image, since information can take many forms. Finally, it seems to me that artistic activity, above and beyond the question of the validity of representation, cannot avoid dealing with the problems of the production and diffusion of information. Faced with the giant monopolies of the information industry, do artists have the means to set up micro information networks?

The critique of the image by the image

The inquiry into the real conducted by 90s' artists took as its model the information produced daily by anonymous operatives on behalf of international news agencies. In this case the photograph was at its simplest, devoid of any stylistic effects apart from those associated with a certain generic image that was delivered in a continuous stream via teletype and Internet servers, and stored later in image banks. By co-opting this non-subjective (if not objective) form of the standard informational image, the artist became a semi-automatic producer, someone apparently content to document the many events that shape our world.

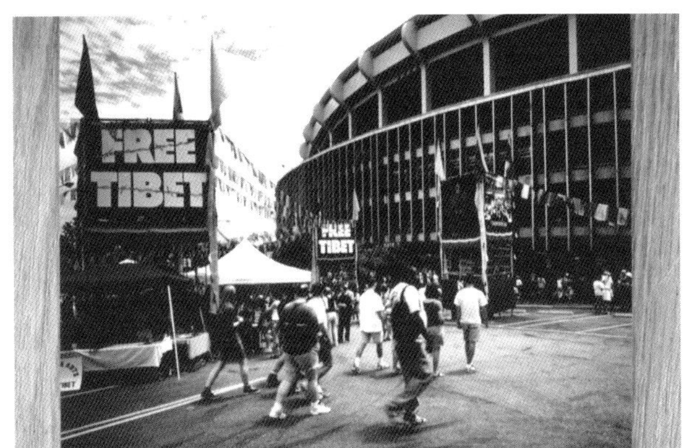

Bruno Serralongue: *Free Tibet*, Washington DC, (série *Free Tibet*)
cibachrome, 127 x157 cm
courtesy Air de Paris

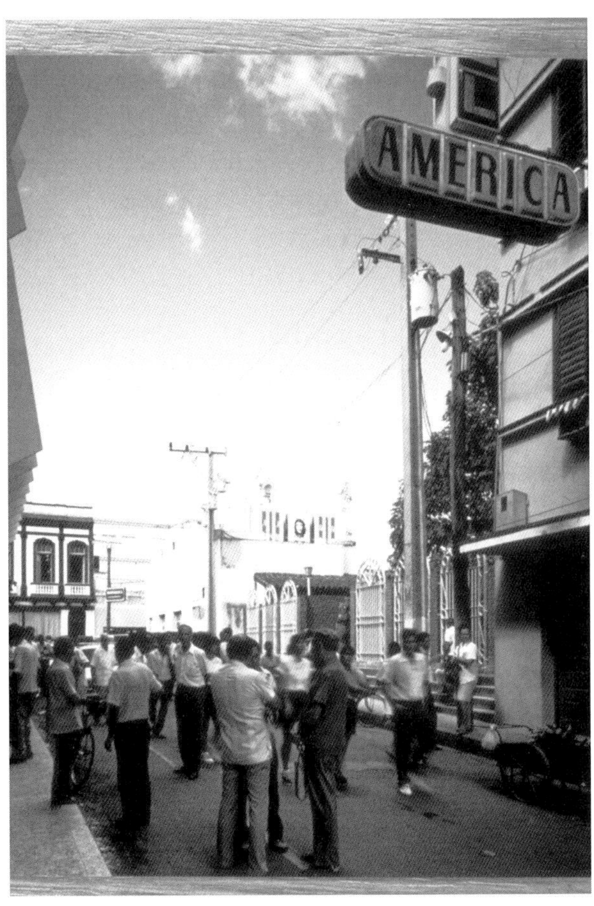

Bruno Serralongue: *Portrait of Ernesto Guevara, Santa Clara, 16 10 97*, 1997
cibachrome, 153 x 123 cm
courtesy Air de Paris

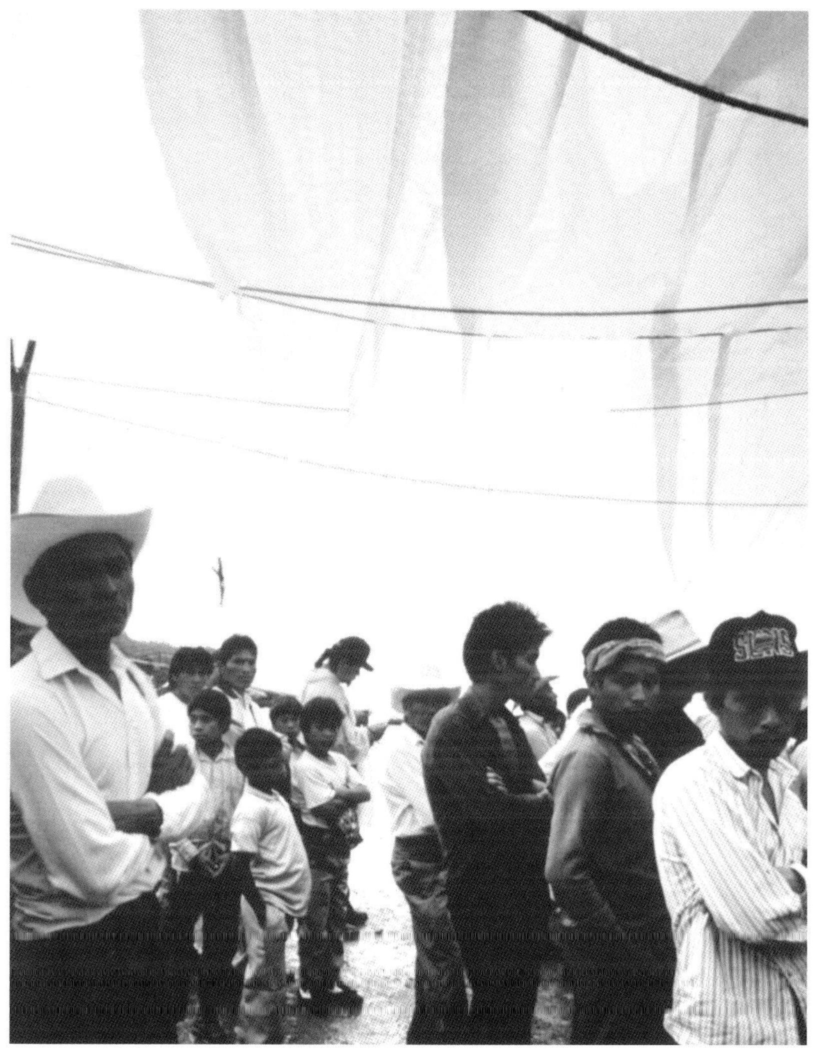

Bruno Serralongue: *Indians*, (chiapas) 1996
cibachrome, 158,5 x 129 cm
courtesy Air de Paris

In the early 90s, with their project entitled *Documents*, Liam Gillick and Henry Bond developed a rigorous method that left no room at the outset for any subjectivity. In each country where they happened to find themselves, they visited the scenes of events announced as news items through the wire services of the press agencies. The automatism they imposed on themselves not only enabled them to avoid choosing the subjects of their photographs, but also produced a hetergeneous body of current images, thereby reconstructing daily reality as it is determined by journalists. Not reality *per se*, but one possible reality. By doing this, they brought out the undeniable fact that the world as we know it is constructed daily by professionals, in accordance with obscure selection criteria. And by contextualizing their work on information at various points throughout the world, they made it clear that there are *many different kinds* of current events, and that these make up a corresponding number of realities. One and the same fact can be crucially important in a given country or region, yet be devoid of interest elsewhere. Although they forced themselves to follow the working procedures of journalists, the artists did not have access to the codes of representation that determined their images. The point was, then, to produce another type of current event using images different from those of the professionals, which are evaluated in accordance with a whole set of editorial imperatives.

The working techniques of reporters, whose movements and production are subject to the vicissitudes of day-to-day events, can also be employed within the framework of a unique and copious research effort that sees the world through the filter of an obsessional subject. Inquiry, in this case, tends towards a certain exhaustiveness. This holds for Christopher Draeger's *Voyages apocalyptiques* [Apocalyptic Voyages] (1994-1995), which travels around the world to document, after the fact, the places where certain modern day disasters occurred. Like an investigative journalist, Draeger visited the sites of collective and historical dramas. From the World Trade Centre in New York to the Heysel Stadium in Brussels, and from Cape Canaveral to Kobe, his successive voyages have drawn an *Apocalyptic Map of the World*. If there can be no answers to his questions about the laws of chance, his photographs, which are done in a casual or nondescript manner, do not cast light on events; rather, a factual text accompanying each image gives a brief description of the catastrophe and details its human and financial costs. The discrepancy between these pictures of innocuous places and the descriptions of the ills that have gone on in them reinforces the impression that the photograph is very often only a false witness, incapable of saying anything more than what reality sets before us in appearances.

In the early phases of his work, Bruno Serralongue concerned himself with those many daily micro catastrophes that newspapers indiscriminately place in the category of "news in brief," or trivial events. This zero degree of journalism dealing with the infra-ordinary is the subject of Serralongue's *Faits divers* [News in Brief] series, which he executed between 1993 and 1995 using fillers found in the French regional newspaper, *Nice-Matin*. Serralongue's procedures have enabled him to produce images regularly, while freeing him from the necessity to make choices or decisions. He reads the paper each day and, with a press clipping as his only clue, goes looking for the place where the event he has read about happened. Then he produces an image, which is invariably empty, or nearly empty, of traces of that event. The places he photographs tend to retain no memory of the dramas that have taken place in them, and the photograph can only attest to its own limits, to its inevitable slowness in the face of the abrupt nature of the events on which daily reality is based. Going back to the basic mechanisms of information fabrication, Serralongue, to contextualize his images, has to act as a rewriter, that link in the chain of print media entrusted with the task of writing photo captions that are, in effect, summaries of the stories on which the photographs are based. The artist shows that it is necessary to articulate both text and image, as a way of bestowing meaning on the latter and legitimating its existence.

These artists who duplicate the professional activities of journalists, reporters and investigators establish a system that completely frees them from the famous author function, which can only be obsolete now that the repertory of attitudes has been exhausted. Instead of attempting to integrate themselves into a history of representation, which is not their subject, they set up an apparatus, a framework within which they can work. (This is very different, of course, from Conceptual Art, which tended to use the trappings of bureaucratic, depersonalized work only to more thoroughly question the foundations of the definition of the work of art.) No psychology is marshalled in their inquiry, nor any irony vis-à-vis the nameless participants in daily life. Rather, the repetitive work of the inquiry brings them into a direct relationship with the real, sometimes even to the point of leading them to intervene concretely as one of its professional agents by blending artistic activity and daily life. Thus, during a residency in Corsica, Bruno Serralongue opted to work for a month as an anonymous photojournalist for the regional daily, *Corse-Matin*. The pictures he published during this time, which illustrated articles on local issues, eventually came to constitute an independent body of work. As it was, the artist conferred the task of selection indirectly on his editor-in-chief.[3] The framework of a professional activity enabled the artist to question his ability to actually put the real into perspective. The decision-making structures of professionals operating within civil society were used not only as models, but also as the effective means of a *critique of the image by the image*–to employ the expression of Pierre Bourdieu.

The artist as operator

This critique also revealed the concrete processes involved in the fabrication of the image. This trial of information manufacturing was informed by an acknowledged experience of its constitutive principles. An essential fact in the stated choices of 90s' artists, and one that has governed their activity, resides in the bold idea of an order which they give themselves. Contradicting the artist's mythic "liberty," these artists have become simultaneously bosses and employers. Hence Serralongue's statement:

[3] See Bruno Serralongue, *Concernant quelques événements de ces dernières années* (FRAC Corsica: Corte, 1998).

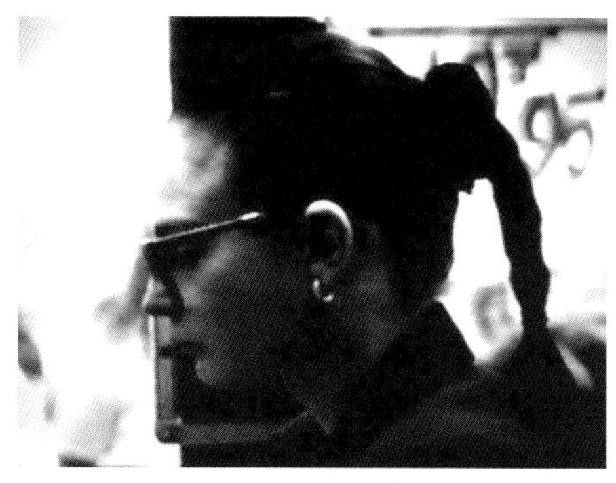
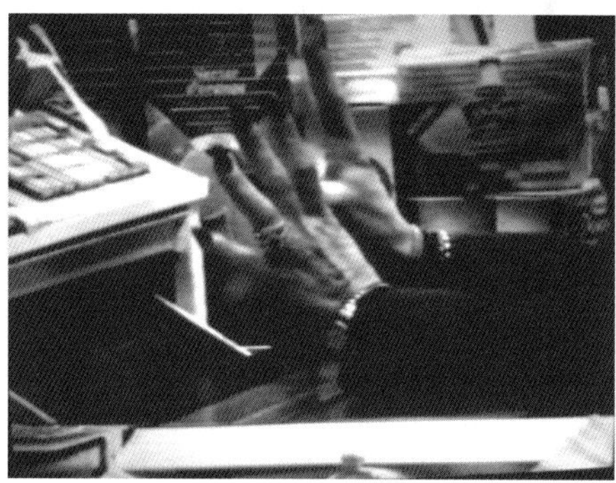
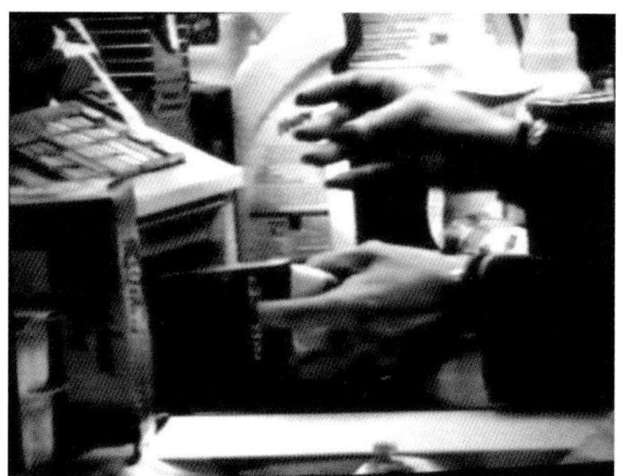
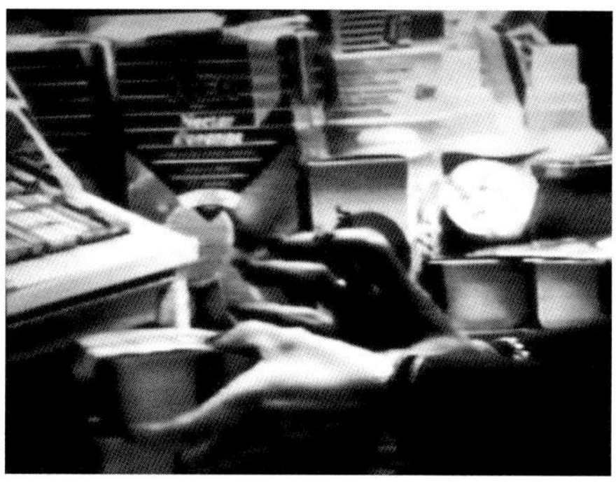

Pierre Faure/Marie-Francine Le Jalu
La Pesanteur et la Grâce,
1997
© Plans Fixes

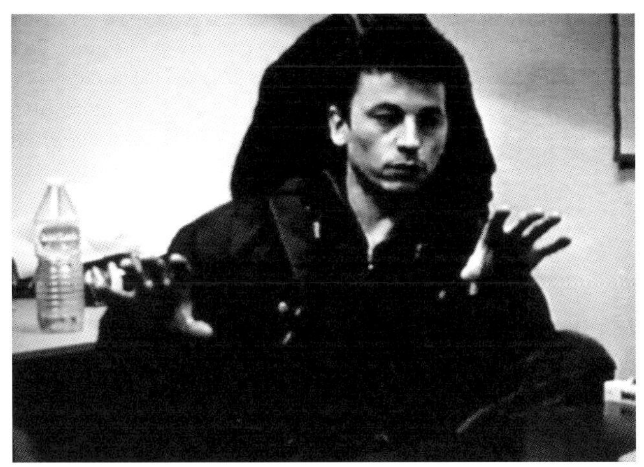

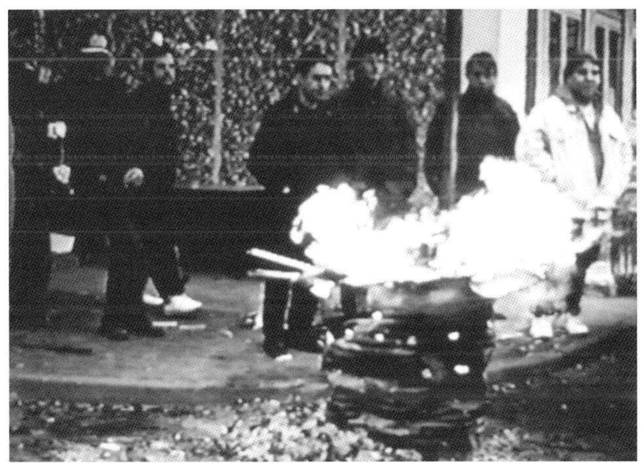

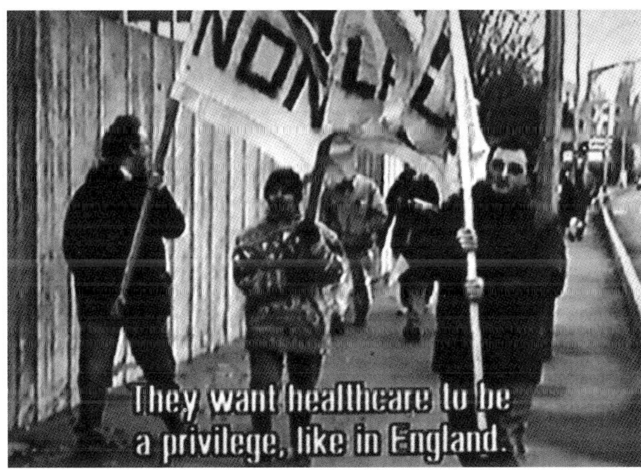

Pierre Faure:
Quelques jours en decembres,
1996
© Plans Fixes

The general framework of my work can be summed up by [the idea of] an order [given]. [...] It is essential to integrate this idea into my photographs. In the circumstances, I am talking about orders that I give to myself, but this is how I really see them; since I think that we are touching on ontology, the foundation of photography, which for me is something impersonal. The operator is not necessarily the most important element in photographic practice.[4]

Since 1996, Bruno Serralongue has developed this command strategy within the context of a global project that has lead him to directly confront the conditions governing the production and diffusion of informational images. By travelling regularly to the sites of major political and media events, he has observed that access to the mediatized real is confined to "image professionals." His photographs result, therefore, from a certain number of constraints and from his ability to adapt to them. Kept by various police authorities from entering the sphere accessible to photojournalists, he intervenes on the margins of events. He has made the observation that representations of the real are tailored in advance. Working in the darkroom, a tool ill suited to snapshots, he has had to choose a fixed viewpoint and limit the number of images produced. In Chiapas, he devoted as much time to the stage-managed appearances of rebel leader Marcos as he did to the Indians and their surroundings. In Las Vegas, he made portraits of French workers, fans of Johnny Hallyday. In Hong Kong during the handing back of the city to China, he photographed neighbourhood festivities, publicity

---

[4] Pascal Beausse, "Entretien avec Bruno Serralongue," *Blocnotes*, no. 16 (Winter 1999), pp. 28-39.

stunts and fireworks displays. In Cuba, it was the Cuban people's tribute to Che Guevara, and in Washington the crowd of a large benefit concert that the Beastie Boys organized on behalf of Tibet. Working against the grain of the sensational and the spectacular, Bruno Serralongue photographs different types of current events from the perspective of the nameless individual lost in the crowd.

Protean documentaries

As a tool for in-depth inquiry into specific manifestations of the real, film offers an effective alternative to the inevitably fragmentary image produced by still photography. The codes of documentary film are combined with those of fictional film, reflecting a heightened awareness of the first principle that every attempt to represent reality participates in the stage-managing of that reality. There is nothing gullible about post-documentary artists' films, which draw upon all those resources generally considered to be unusable by documentary film makers who believe in the possibility of *cinéma verité*. As a result, information acquires a hitherto unknown degree of plasticity.

Pierre Faure shows how fiction is central to representations of the real. His use of montage in *La pesanteur et la grâce* [Gravity and Grace] (1997), a film portrait of a supermarket cashier talking about her work experience, combines film narrative techniques deemed to be, *a priori*, heterogeneous. These range from a Godard-like use of slow motion to show a hand picking up a product (the conveyor belt as image editor) to a scene depicting an interview being done on the cashier's house. The cashier speaks in a mechanical manner, using terms suggested by her assimilation of the repetitive gestures required by her job. The symbolic violence that the work world perpetrates on the individual appears all the more glaring in the light of this unconscious acceptance of an automation of life.

The film, *Quelques jours en décembre* [A Few Days in December] (1996), follows the daily lives of workers occupying a central mail-sorting station during the widespread strike that immobilized France in 1995 and relaunched the social movement. The documentary format employed makes time pass slowly, focusing as it does on those dead periods when the strikers exchange ideas in a continual analysis of the evolution of the above-mentioned social movement. The black and white film is made up of sequence shots that reveal, over the course of some eighty minutes, the doubts and confusion of the strikers. Instead of emphasizing the high points of the public demonstrations, Faure makes use of a diluted temporality (in contrast to the constrictive formats of television reports) to simply show how time drags on during work stoppages and how difficult it is to occupy the workplace while resisting appeals to go back to work.

Today's artists do not claim to reconstruct a hypothetical (and mythical) "raw" image of the real. Despite all, however, they do enjoy the possibility of playing upon the different regimes of visibility now available in order to offset the numerous drawbacks in the representations of social reality produced by the omnipotent television image.

The Roumanian revolution and the Gulf War had already come to an end when Serge Daney penned the following statement:

It was at the very time that it became more "high-performance" than ever that televised information, with its news and its magazines, its overplayed restrictions and its overpaid stars, rediscovered a somewhat forgotten truth, namely, that we cannot always film anything in any way we please. Something, something from the side of the real, is resistant to homogenization.

Later on he would add, "There, there is no information."[5]

Recording studios and TV and film sets frequently recur, along with dubbing rooms, as motifs in the work of artists such as Philippe Parreno, Pierre Huyghe and John Miller, reflecting the extent to which audio-visual production facilities have become strategic in the fabrication of the real. In these places where messages are constructed, the stage management of reality knows no limits, taken up as it is in a vast entreprise aimed at the aestheticization of reality. Subverted, the studio becomes an empty stage set, a field for the incription of simulacra.

It is from just such a studio, located in the middle of a large urban centre, that the narrator of Charles de Meaux and Philippe Parreno's *Le pont du trieur* [The Sorter's Bridge] (1999) describes Pamir, a fomer Soviet territory in central Asia. In their words, it is "an area that the West has no image of."[6] Sequences

[5] Serge daney, *Devant la recrudescence des vols de sac à main* (Paris: Aléas éditeur, 1997), p. 146.
[6] The quotes are taken from the press release issued by the production company, Anna Sanders Films (Dijon), for the first screening of this film on June 5, 1999 in Paris.

devoted to the recording of the sound track (shot in a way which suggests that they have been staged) alternate with documentary-style images of the region and its inhabitants. Interviews, city scenes, slow panoramas of mountainous landscape and information about the region's economic and political situation gradually build up a fragmentary picture of Pamir. However, there is also a certain amount of dreamlike footage in which the camera, in a long tracking shot, follows the desert jaunt of four people perched on a motorcycle equipped with a rudimentary side car. A blend of documentary footage and basic history (with characters but no plot), *Le Pont du Trieur* is not an example of docu-fiction but "an informational emission that is gradually transformed into a story." This singular film, which neither a documentary filmmaker nor a director of fictional features would feel authorized to make, attempts to provide a polymorphus image of reality.

Image deficit

With the Gulf War and the crisis in Kosovo as archetypes, major contemporary international crisis are imageless. And what shall we say about conflicts that are either too far away or too complex–East Timor, Massoud's struggle against the Taliban, the Cambodian genocide? In the face of modern history, what does an event that has no images of it made or distributed represent? Has it even taken place? We are familiar with the definitive statement by Jean Baudrillard (articulated before, during and after the Gulf War) denying the existence of the event. Wars, massacres, torture–none of the disgraces of this century exist in the eyes of their contemporaries unless they have been depicted. The validity of this principle is verifiable to the point that it can be extended to events that have been photographed, but whose images do not correspond to the codes or expectations of international audiences. A representation that does not square with the collective mental image of it runs the risk of being rejected and denied.

Liam Gillick and Philippe Parreno have shown, with their exhibition titled *Le procès de Pol Pot*[7] [The Trial of Pol Pot], the symbolic effects of the lack of representation of an event. How can one give an account of an historical fact from the standpoint of art? Gillick and Parreno have opposed documentary procedures with a denial of the image. Instead of gathering a pile of information from that already produced by historians and the media, they have conceived their exhibition space as a huge television studio, as a space where messages could be inscribed as if on the pages of an electronic notepad or a reporter's prompter screen. Apart from the word "Khmer," an ultimate sign, the sentences, words and numbers inscribed on the walls have no apparent relationship to the historical reality on trial here, and on which they are supposedly meant to cast some light. These abstract words reveal the abstruse "forest of signs" constituted by the superimposition each day of information in all shapes and sizes, which comes to us from very different channels with incompatible technological standards. A series of numbers ("11198888333333333") is obviously a piece of

[7] Shown at Le Magasin (a national contemporary art centre in Grenoble) from November 8, 1998 to November 3, 1999.

information, but without the requisite decoder it remains mute, closed in upon itself, *illegible*. *Le Procès de Pol Pot*, planned by the artists even before the sudden announcement of the actual trial, is more than an attempt to suggest a substitute for a *missing image*. For the system of information is also on trial here, not in order to denounce its shortcomings but to prove the inability of the "global network" to represent the event. Thus our ability to judge the real without recourse to the image is put forward as an issue for debate.

Reality hackers

An artist wishing to function as more than an extra within the real might very well find that the information infrastructure, a veritable locus of world power, is a strategic place to launch an attack.

Gianni Motti is a hacker who targets reality. He appropriates sensational events by calling news agencies and, like a terrorist, claiming responsibility for them. In the wake of a call that Motti made to Agence france presse, in which he claimed that he was responsible for an earthquake that had just occurred, the news agency circulated a dispatch. Like a virus, the artist reconfigures global networks for his own purposes, slips into their constant stream of data and assigns the nameless scribes of the news agencies the task of drafting the documents that attest to the effectiveness of his "performance."

The members of the Szuper Gallery collective have let themselves into empty offices and television studios of the

Bloomberg financial information chain to leave a nominal human trace inside this technological Moloch with its news flashes and its continual scroll of digital signals conveying the ups and downs of international stock exchanges. In the video, *Contemporary Art* (1998), a TV broadcast studio with its phalanx of computer screens and other electronic display panels seemed to function as a closed circuit, justifying its existence through the continuous production, twenty-four hours a day, of abstract information in rapid flux that nonetheless affects the courses of millions of lives.

The discrepancy between the virtualization of information and the density of the corresponding human experience only reveals, in a colder light, how the electronic spectacle takes away the individual's ability to run his own life.

New media

The emergence of new information technologies and the rapid expansion of this dominant model within the framework of a "cyberrevolution" has tapped into the string of fantasies of a "utopia of communication"[8]–to use Philippe Breton's apt expression. Out of all these fantasies, the least effect of which is not a confusion between actual facts and their representation, the most recent to be promoted to the status of flavour of the month identifies the individual as a "machine that commu-nicates."[9] The most ridiculous example of this new manifesta-

[8] Philippe Breton, *L'utopie de la communication* (Paris: La Découverte, 1997).
[9] *Ibid*, p. 156.

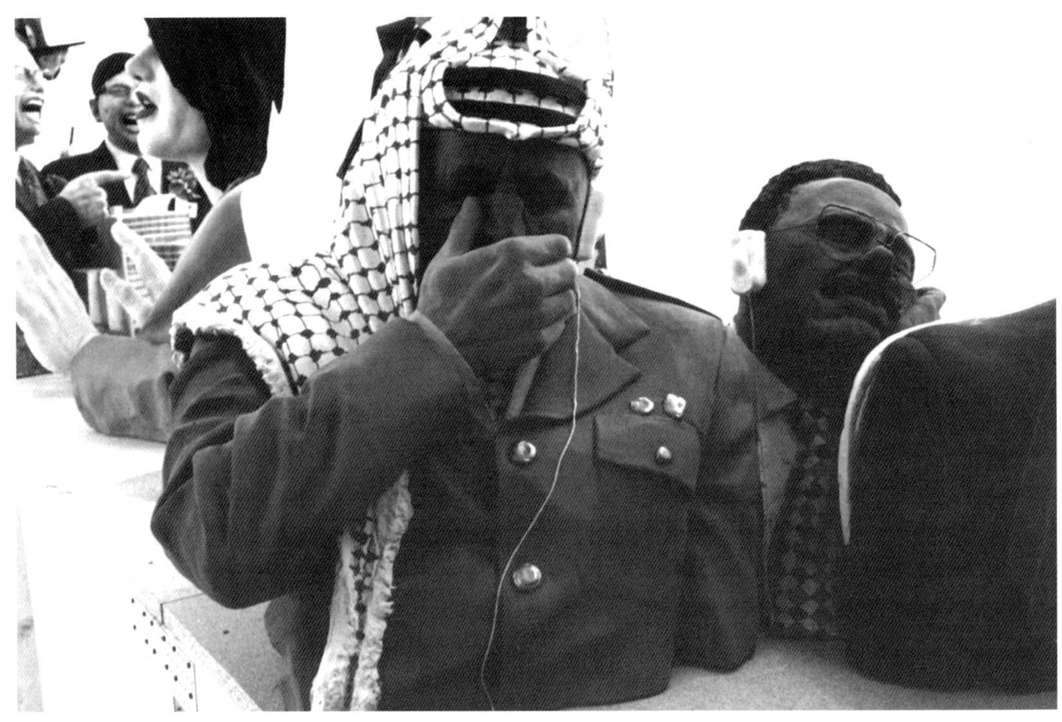

Wang Du: *Marché aux puces -Mise en vente d'informations d'occasion*, 1999
(detail)
Courtesy Art & Public, Genève

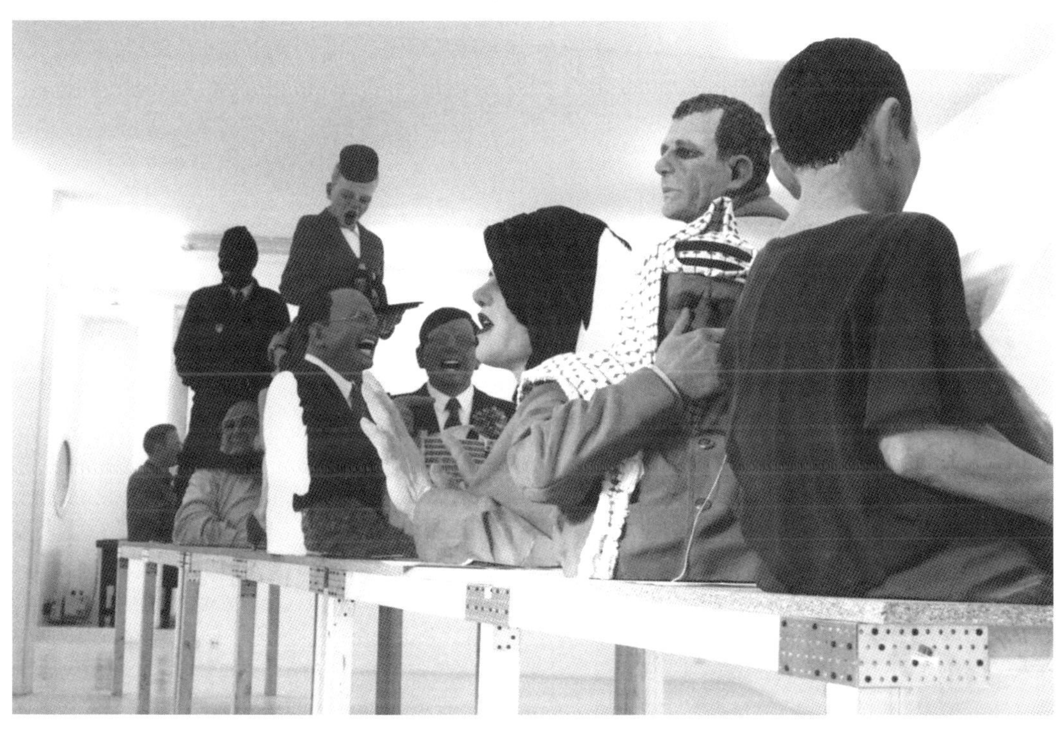

Wang Du: *Marché aux puces- Mise en vente d'informations d'occasion*, 1999
Courtesy Art & Public, Genève

tion of individualism to appear in our so called "postmodern" societies is personified in the figure of Matt Drudge. Through the agency of his Internet site, *The Drudge Report*, he literally shortcircuited the traditional media by being the first to uncover the "sex scandal" that led to "Monicagate." According to Ignacio Ramonet, the Clinton-Lewinski affair, originally attributed to information overload, can henceforth be considered as "the founding event of new information media."[10]

Baptised *self-media*, such new media are defined as individual, autonomous entities that function outside the professional sphere of the mass media and diffuse information on the worldwide web from personal computers. The expansion of this new model of cybernetic guerilla journalist could overload and jam the information system, and could also be a threat to the "classical" profession of journalist. According to this new paradigm, each individual would potentially correspond to a media source. "Each individual could, theoretically, become a global media source and a competitor of CNN."[11] It is easy to see the danger to democracy that such a new Tower of Babel would represent.

However, one must be wary of extreme likes or dislikes when dealing with this phenomenon. On the one hand, we must remember that the concept of self-media originally appeared in the early 1970s, well before widespread access to the Internet (which, by the way, originated within the American military industrial complex of the 1960s, at the height of the Cold War.

[10]. Ignacio Ramonet, *La Tyrannie de la communication* (Paris: Galilée, 1999).
[11] Ignacio Ramonet, *Libération*, Friday, April 16, 1999.

What strange utopia is this that has its cradle in the Pentagon!)[12] On the other hand, we should measure the emergence of this new media model against the crisis currently underway among the traditional media, which have come to be seen as vile in this era of real suspicion. If we leave aside its most extreme contemporary manifestations and refer instead to the original concept formulated by Jean Cloutier in 1973,[13] the notion of self-media becomes quite interesting. Divested of technological paraphernalia, this idea represents the possibility for truly personal exchanges at a time when human communication is becoming ever more difficult.

The artist's transformation into media

In his "entrepreneurial" take on artistic activity, Andy Warhol was certainly a pioneer of media production activity in the sphere of art. We must remember–his *Journal* does a good job of reconstructing his daily obsession with the idea–that the quasi-mechanical production of paintings by assistants in his aptly named Factory (a transposition of Taylorism to the artistic activity of society portraiture), was geared toward the capitalist objective of giving Warhol the means to carry out his activities as press boss (with *Interview* magazine) and as the creator, producer and host of a show for cable TV (*Andy Warhol's Fifteen Minutes*, followed by *Andy Warhol's TV*).

[12] On this point, see particularly Manuel Castells, *La société en réseaux - l'ère de l'information* (Paris: Fayard, 1998), p. 71 and pp. 392-393.
[13] Cf. Patrick Thomas, *Libération*, Friday, April 2, 1999.

Twenty years after Warhol's brand of television, with the television industry expanding exponentially to the point where it is the main player in an information-based style of show business, there seems to be little room for artists on its channels, unless they feature as curiosities at the service of endless entertainment.

Of course there is always the possibility of pirate activity, like that developed after 1995 by Pierre Huyghe. *Mobil TV* is a local itinerant television station that places a control room, set and transmission system at the disposal of its users, who themselves make up its programming schedule. Huyghe defines it as a "point of departure for shared social time, an alternative to the work/time-off rhythm and the reified exchange it suggests." And he continues by giving what could undoubtedly serve as a definition of his research:

What conditions are required for one to be part of an image, an image in which one can move about, one that does not exclude the viewer but positions him as an actor, an image that produces feedback, a connecting image in which each person can decide how much time he wants to spend with it? This time shared with the image is the reality of the image.

The viewer simultaneously becomes actor, producer and receiver of his own TV programs (which are broadcast locally) by breaking out of the consumer passivity to which he is usually confined by commercial television. Pierre Huyghe thus authorizes citizens to take control of images of their reality.

Beginning in the early 1980s, Tetsuo Kogawa developed his *Mini-FM* system. Operating as a micro guerilla media unit, he distributed small FM radio wave transmitters throughout an urban environment. Although the transmitters are not very powerful, they are so close together that it is possible to broadcast citywide, circumventing all legal systems. Thus Tetsuo Kogawa has created a truly independent radio station in Tokyo, referring to Félix Guattari's writings on free populist radio.[14] Committed to this movement in Japan, each time he gives a lecture he explains how simple and inexpensive it is to build a transmitter. In a workshop entitled *How to build a one-watt FM transmitter*, he begins by demonstrating how to make a unit in very little time and then suggests to volunteers, be they individuals or members of associations, that they in turn make their own mini-FM units and establish alternative programming. The fluency of radio is Kogawa's response to the heaviness of television.

In 1994 Chris Burden was invited to mount an exhibition at the Le Consortium art centre in Dijon. In response, he created a small video journal by setting up a low-tech news network modelled on the ancient system of town criers. A fleet of Citroen vans (2Cvs) was outfitted with television screens and sent out along the roads of the Burgundy region. The arrival of these news vans in village squares was quite an event. People appeared with folding chairs and made themselves comfortable behind the vehicles, where they sat under canvas awnings. This "video circus" showed a continuous montage of images of disasters that had occurred in California, from the Los Angeles riots to earthquakes, fires and the looting of stores and

---

[14] Tetsuo Kogawa, *Toward a Polymorphous Radio*,
http://anarchy.k2.tku.ac.jp/anarchy98/radio/micro/radiorethink.html

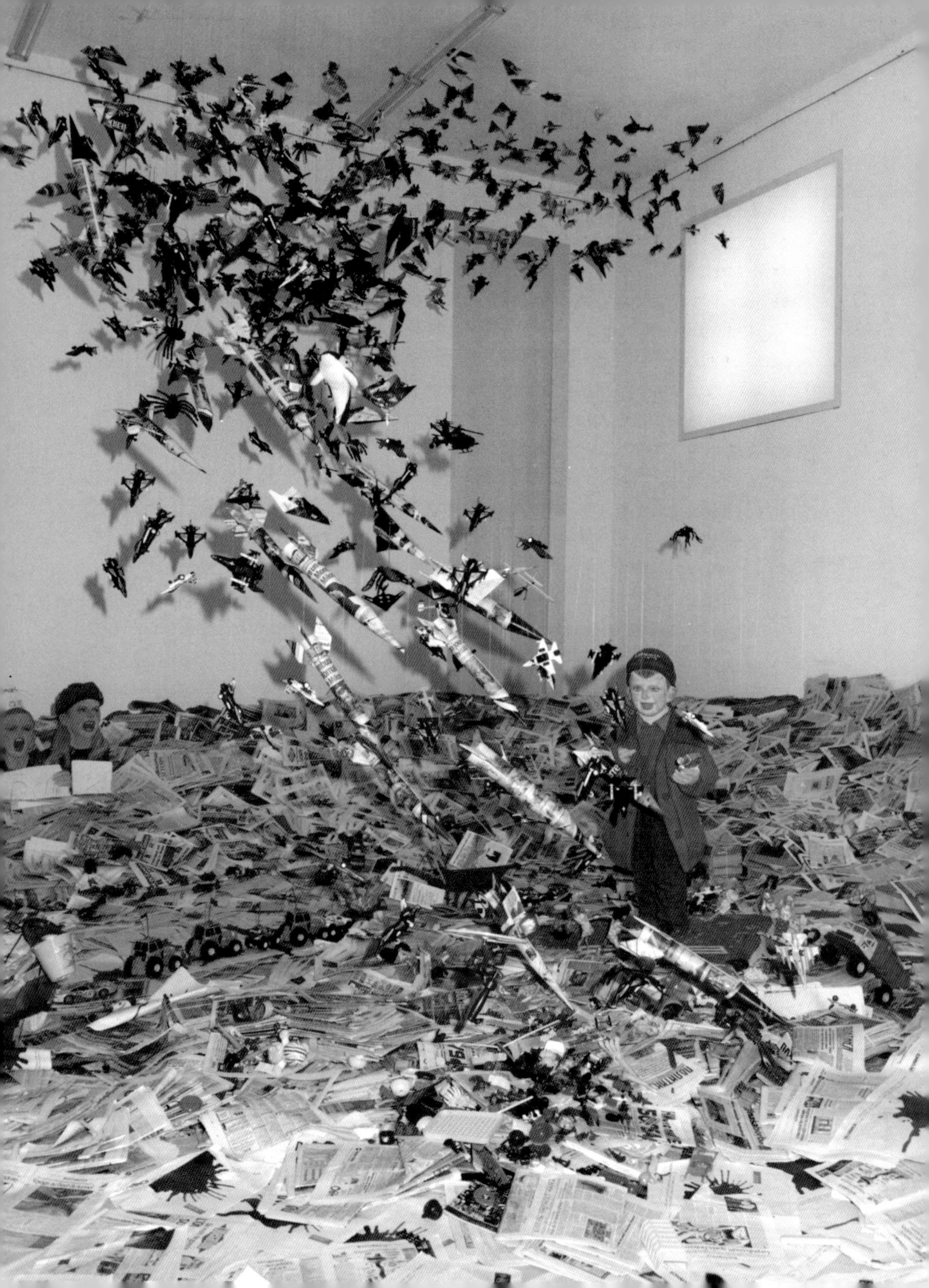

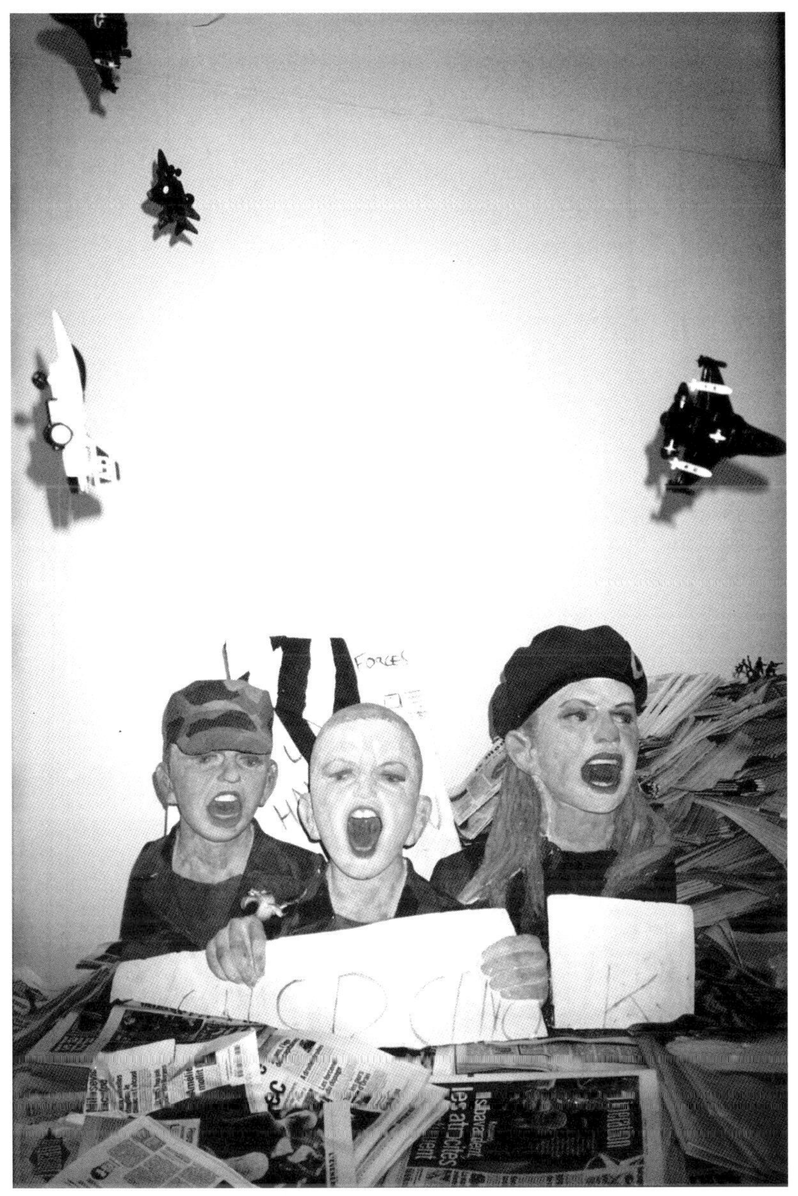

Wang Du: *Stratégie en Chambre*, 1999
view of the exhibition ´Dial M For…` Kunstverein, Munich (3 juillet -15 août 1999)
Courtesy galerie Art & Public, Genève
Ph: Stephen Rault

businesses. This catastrophist vision of the social reality of a region characterized by its latent violence reproduced the deluge of sensationalist images seen on specialized TV channels that continually broadcast millenarian messages over American cable networks. With its single subject and its play upon a tiny, archaic form of news service, Burden's *News from California and Around the World* showed how our perception of current events can be biased by the editorial choices of the broadcasters. While he undermined the American dream by showing its darkest side, Burden also played on the idea of information as a closed circuit, one calibrated, in his encoding, on cinematographic and TV fictions that chip away a little more each day at the relationship to the world of citizens captivated by the trailers of sensationalistic news stories.

Post reality

Wang Du is a paradigm of the self-media artist. Given the degree to which reality is overrepresented, today's artists enjoy the possibility of duplicating information. But by transforming the immateriality of media images into a very concrete materiality, Wang Du does more than situate the flood of information within an endless progression or *mise en abîme*; rather, he transmits its virtuality into the real. If the idea of "post reality" has anything interesting to recommend it, it would be the premise that it sets up a new equation for reality, one that was produced in the era of global information and that says that if there is no image, there is no reality.

Wang Du makes plaster sculptures based on images picked up from the world press and the Internet. In their passage from a two-dimensional state to a three-dimensional one, these images retain their initial framing as well as the distortions produced by the camera lens. Above and beyond the reality effect produced by the transposition of flat images into volumes, Wang Du's sculptures, which he paints with gouache, are incisive comments on our era. His installations effect a spectacular intrusion of figures associated with public events or various types of scandals into the real space of the exhibition. With *Marché aux Puces—mise en vente d'informations d'occasion* [Flea Market—Sale of Second-hand Information] (1999), Wang Du has created a grotesque parade of both nameless and famous individuals. Eleven sculptures are laid out along a long table, as if in a stall. Confined to the same plane and conforming to non-hierarchical scales, they reproduce the equalization of events brought about by the media. The visual compression suggested by their arrangement in succession points to the lack of differentiation that prevails in today's print media and television. A handshake between presidents Li-Peng and Chirac is set against three other hands busy fitting a condom over an erect penis. Yasser Arafat drowses during a meeting of the United Nations, while Monica replies to questions from journalists. This crush of people reproduces the commotion and vulgarity of the media, the daily indigestion of the glut of information.

By combining very different images ranging from historical events to sidebar trivia, from staged trash TV to the people photographs of the paparazzi, Wang Du shows how interchangeable

public figures have become at a time when information has
become a product.

Artists as self-media

Wang Du has been programmatic, declaring: "I want to be a
media source." He sees himself as "a journalist after the fact."
According to this unusual proposition, the artist becomes a
producer of recycled information picked up from the visual
material available through the mass media.

How can artistic activity deal with history in the making?
Manet already faced this challenge with his painting, *The
Execution of Emperor Maximillian*. Although dated 1867, the
year of the event, the painting was actually made between 1868
and 1869, as a sort of competitive gesture in the direction of
photography. Wang Du does not participate in this race (which,
in any case, is already lost) between art and information. He is,
on the contrary, full aware of the inevitable delay of
representation in relation to the real, which is all the more
evident when it is not carried out with the tools and connections
of professional journalists. Thus when he decided, at the
beginning of the war in Kosovo, to do a piece dealing with the
way in which the media dealt with the war while it was still
going on, he did not set out to describe how the events unfolded
or to explain their geopolitical context. *Stratégie en chambre*
[Armchair Strategist] (1999) was shown for the first time at the
Basel Art Fair just after the war ended.

Wang Du brings the most searing and close-to-home current events into a room sheltered from the noise of the world. Placed atop an imposing mass of several tons of newspapers published throughout the world during the war in Kosovo, three sculptures sum up the phenomenon of media frenzy. The disenchanted figures of Clinton and Yeltsin, "rulers" of a world that has not mourned its partition into two blocs, face a Serbian child posing gallantly on the wing of a downed F-117 aircraft. A third sculpture features a group of three pro-NATO Albanian children demonstrating in military fatigues. Overlooking the installation, an armada of toys represent the hail of weapons that descended on Serbia and Kosovo.

Placed in the midst of an ocean of newspapers, these iconic figures, which are more anecdotal figures than true representations of History, make use of absurdity to illustrate the hollowness of journalistic information, of its ability to fill up space daily so as to more effectively mask the bankruptcy of its claim to objectivity. During the entire period of the conflict, there were no images to tell us what was actually going on inside Kosovo's borders. Like the pictures of missiles hitting their targets, recirculating the artificial idea of a clean war conducted like a video game, the thousands of photographs contained in the newspapers that Wang Du collected can only contribute to a weakening of our relationship to the world. This communication madness, which grips the media throughout the world on the occasion of historical (or even anedcotal) events, is exactly what Wang Du is talking to us about. In other words, the fatuousness and sterility of information.

His bold wish to function as new media with the limited means available to the artist makes Wang Du a pioneer in this unheard-of conception of the artist. Critiquing the volatility of information by making it more densely material, he anticipates the effects we can expect when images are made three dimensional–a development already announced by the advertising industry. In the era of virtual information, the danger of a communicational flood has given shape to the idea of an invasion of all available real space by informational material.

Toward an actualization of the space of the real

The recent deregulation issuing from non-professional journalistic activity on the worldwide web has proven that the only possible result one can expect from the widespread adoption of irresponsible self-media attitudes is a general scrambling of the message and increased confusion in the relationship to the world. This is undoubtedly the point at which the role of the artist assumes its full significance as a mediator between the real and the receiver. The artist as self-media, and as the producer and transmitter of alternate information about reality, rebels against the distractions that flow from an ideology of immediacy. The inevitable delay between a given current event and its representation within the sphere of art makes it possible to resist the levelling and deadening effects of the culture industry. By bringing out its non-reflexivity and its automatisms, a critique of the media image makes it possible to break the spell of the spectacle.

When artists break out of their role as simple producers of images and objects–which are never immune to a blunting of their critical (or even subversive) edge by consumer reflexes –they become, as it were, smugglers who give viewers the tools they need to seize control of the means used to produce the visual, acoustic and mental images of their world. The actualization of the various levels of reality contained in daily life, a development brought about by citizens transformed into transmitters and receivers, would make such citizens veritable *participants* in the real. It would then become possible to move beyond passive consumption toward a shaping of the experience of the real, in close contact with its material density. The declaration of such a revolution in the traditional one-way circuit of transmission would undoubtedly have something utopic about it–because, first of all, art could not produce the fiction of a world in which each person has the desire to act on information. The establishment of the conditions of true feedback between the real and its representations is not the artist's right or privilege, but his *work*.

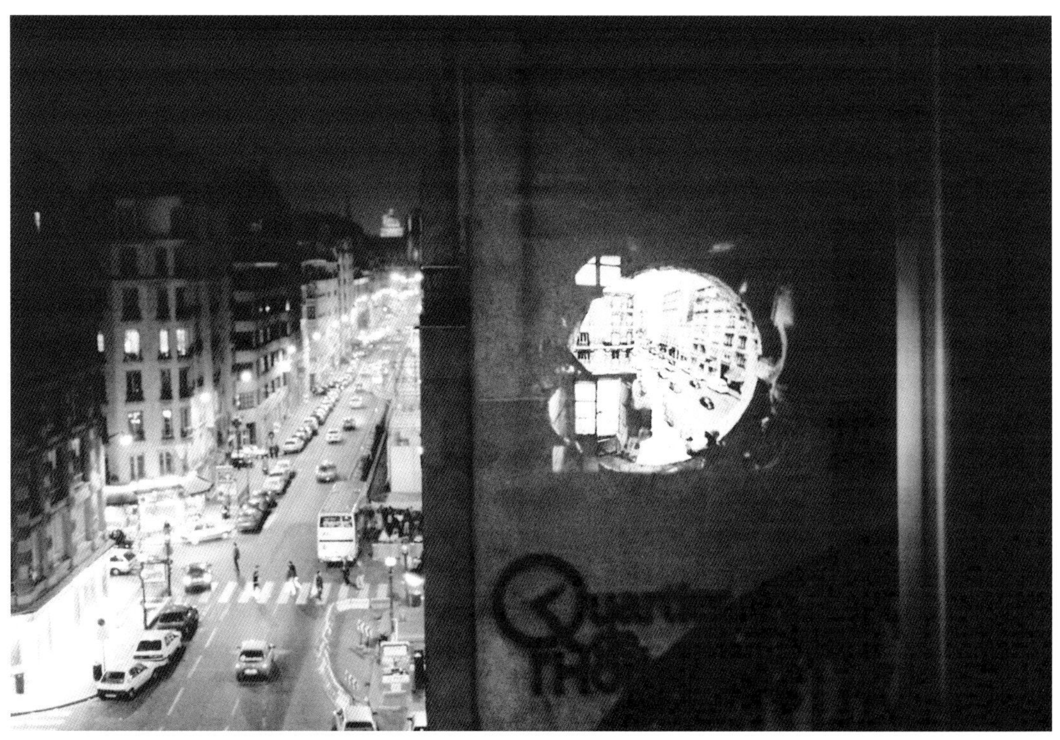

Pierre Huyghe: *Light Conical Intersect*, 1996
Projection of *Conical Intersect* - Gordon Matta Clark 75
Event/Poster

"Deceptual Art":
Contemporary Art as Coproduction

Not meeting expectations—such, if we had to name it, might be the common denominator of contemporary practices. Recycling, copying,[1] replaying[2] and mediating[3] are all forms of practice that buck the demand for preformatted production, a demand that contemporary art can no longer satisfy. Enough of novelty, originality, form/content relations and the cult of the formally finished object! To go on applying these inappropriate criteria of aesthetic evaluation, to maintain certainties as to what art should or should not be, is to impose an increasingly rigid discourse of power and to ignore artists' radical refusal to continue with ill-adapted rules, a refusal violently expressed in practices that are themselves extremist: Henrik Plenge Jacobsen sparking a riot in Copenhagen by

[1] Gilles Barbier copying pages from the dictionary. See Jean-Yves Jouannais' *Artistes sans œuvre* (Paris: Hazan, 1997).
[2] In *Fresh Acconci* (1995) Mike Kelley and Vito Acconci used mannequins to replay the performances of Vito Acconci.
[3] Artists create moments or objects that generate sociability. One thinks of Rirkrit Tiravanija's canteens, as well as other practices discussed by Nicolas Bourriaud in *L'Esthétique relationnelle* (Paris: Les presses du réel, 1998).

installing an overturned bus; Philippe Meste attacking an aircraft carrier and Maurizio Cattelan burgling the Bloom Gallery in Amsterdam in order to "finance" a group show (Another Fucking Ready-made, 1996 at the De Appel Foundation).

So, not meeting expectations. Not because they can't but because they want to have done with all the stereotypes surrounding the artistic, to destroy preconceptions and other forms of received wisdom that freeze the viewer's relation to the work. The position asserted by these artists throws the idea of the artist as *auteur* into crisis, and with it the discourse of power that yokes together stability and the cult of the self. And it does so in order to invent a contemporary relation to the artistic practices of the '90s, to avoid the trap of totalitarian works, as epitomized by the (in every sense) *finished* objects of Jeff Koons,[4] which embody an almost paranoid will to knowledge. A constant feature of Koons' work is the conspicuous reflective power of the materials he uses. Whether in stainless steel (*Rabbit*, 1986), window glass (*One Ball Total Equilibrium*, 1985), glass (*Mound of Flowers*, 1991) or mirror glass (*Wishing Well*, 1988), the surface reflects the viewer—more, it annexes them, just as it does the exhibition space, the other works on display, etc. These polished surfaces express the absurd hypertrophy of work that is increasingly monumental (the inflated dimensions of *Puppy*), coupled with its constitutive capacity to *comprehend* everything, in every sense of that word. The work monumentalizes kitsch and functions here as a kind of reservoir, a commonplaceness that swallows up the viewer. This is an

---

[4] Readers will have understood that I am not attacking Koons' remarkable and stimulating work here, but spelling out what it implies in terms of the position and activity of the viewer.

exercise in annexation which asserts that nothing else exists outside itself, since it is capable of containing and circumscribing everything else, and thus of defining it all in terms of its own power over it. Contained, held at the surface of the work, viewers observe the ravished weakness of their image, a mere reflection, and thus the spectacle of the metaphorization of a role accorded by a work over which they have no control. Koons' tautological art radicalizes the traditional position of the viewer in that it accomplishes it, standing as a metaphor of an absolute knowingness. There is little viewers can do when confronted with this object that casts them aside, that, in the etymological sense, seduces them.

Not to meet expectations, to disappoint them, is to demand here and now that the position of the viewer be reconsidered, that the viewer be repositioned and become the subject, in both the objective and subjective senses—the subject who, in the mismatch between the response offered by the artist and their work discovers not only the impossibility of rehearsing their convictions (the essential legitimacy of art as something founded on novelty, originality, universality, etc.) but also an opportunity to experience the artistic event in a productive mode. It is here, in the refusal to offer a "suitable" response to the viewer's preconceptions, that we can observe the "deceptual"[5] strategy of contemporary practices that engage the viewer in the productive dynamic of the work to come.

[5] The neologism "deceptual" should be read as a combination of "deceptive" with "perceptual" and a negative form of conceptual. A "deceptual" work is one that may both deceive and/or disappoint the viewer.

Pierre Huyghe: *Mobil TV* (95-97), "set (2)"

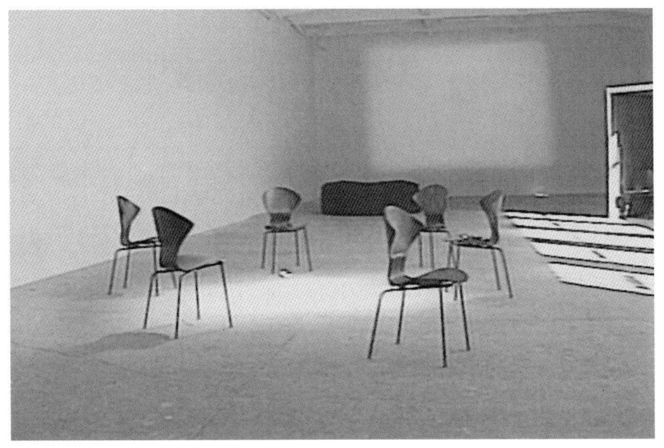

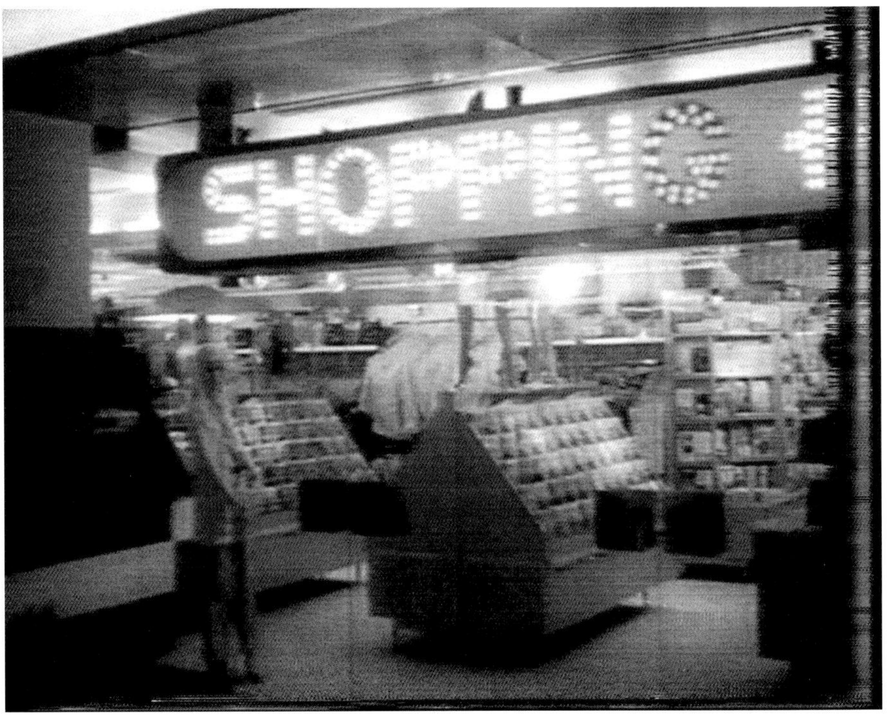

Pierre Huyghe: *Mobil TV* (95-97), " shopping (Debord)"

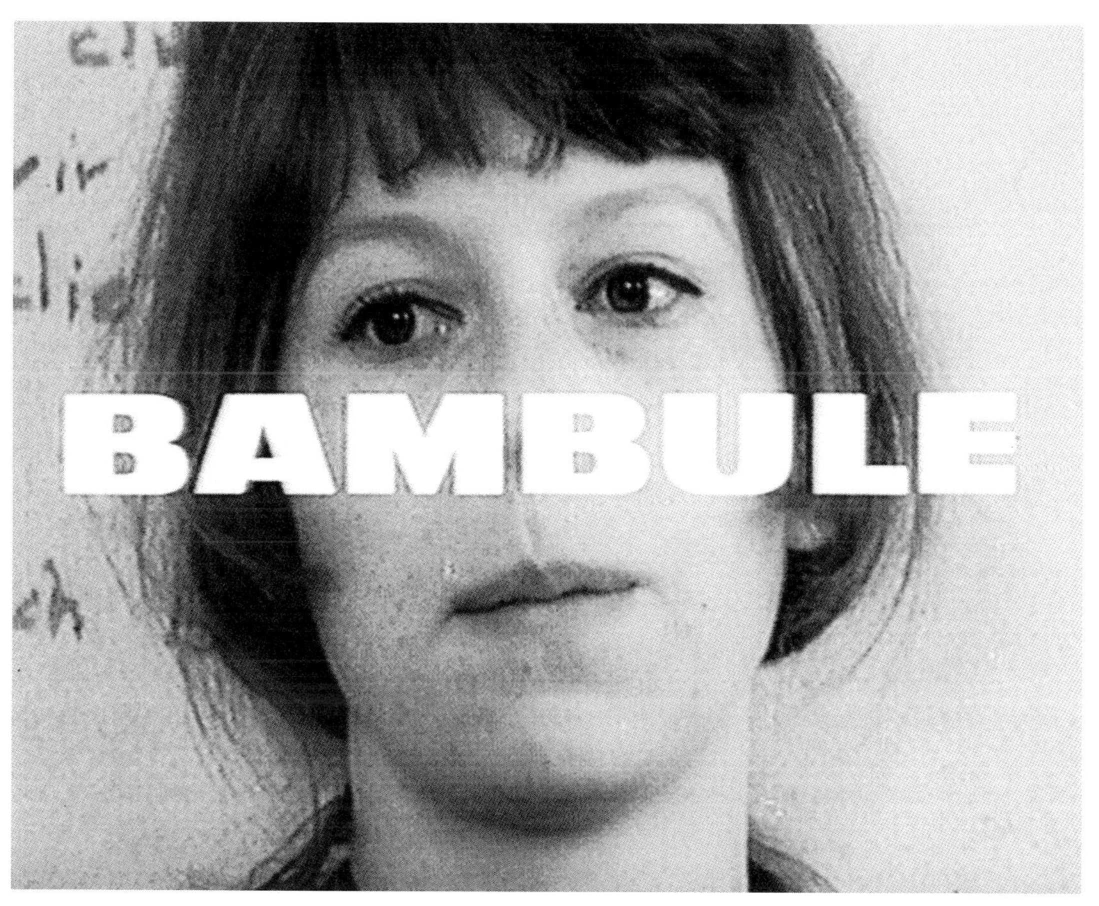

Pierre Huyghe: *Mobil TV*, "Bambule (Meinhof)", 95 97

The artist's aura deficiency

Every viewer attending to an artwork formulates an expectation that they seek to verify, to satisfy, to have fulfilled. This demand on the part of the viewer places every artist—and every artwork—in the position of the one supposed to know, possessing something that motivates and justifies their demand. This transposition of the Lacanian term "supposed subject of knowledge" (*sujet supposé savoir*) into the artistic context helps to make clear what is happening here. The work and, by the effect of transitivity, the artist, are seen as possessing some knowledge that the viewer must tease out, like the figure in the carpet, a knowledge posited as an enigma that they must elucidate in order to enjoy it. On this account, the work is the place where the artist's knowledge is accomplished. Now, however, artists are refusing to take responsibility for this knowledge supposed by the viewer. They are breaking with the authorial persona, the figure of the demiurge, while at the same time refusing to hide behind an absence of signature or any other naive strategy of anonymity. The artist does not seek to disappear, but to question their responsibility with regard to the expectations of the contemporary viewer.

It is the renunciation of such knowledge that informs Ingrid Luche's databases (Villa Arson, Nice, 1997) with their series of dates, highlights of the Cannes Film Festival, family tree of Monaco's ruling house, the Grimaldis, and names of divers celebrities. Judging by the various arrows drawn between different items, this effusive muddle seems to be ordered according to rules as tenuous as they are artificial, such as the coincidences of dates, recurrences of names, etc. But the organizational principles set in motion by the artist soon run out of steam and undercut any totalizing strategy that would hope for and believe in a rational ordering of the multifarious information. At this point, the viewer feels it is their mission to continue the work abandoned by the artist, to fill in the blanks, to choose between different meanings, to go on with the myth of the open work; it is for them, now, to find the meaning of the work. This is an illusion. For once the artist gives up the attempt to organize everything into a whole, a significant truth that calls out to be articulated, then their work becomes the history of this defeat of meaning. Not in a cynical way, though: the point is not to prohibit meaning but to prevent it from being the keystone of the work. This withdrawal implies a deficiency of aura on the part of the artist, who now cuts a most unlikely figure as this supposed subject of knowledge that the viewer wishes them to embody. Ingrid Luche asks that we observe her own deficiency, and experience it. The meaning is to be found not in the ordering of dates in the work on show, but in the renunciation of the certitude of a preexisting knowledge. This shift points up that of the decentered work, a work that resides not in what is presented on the walls, but in the necessarily deceptual use of the situation.

The decentered work

Faced with the urgency of the demands made upon it, the decept proposes a displacement of knowing which cannot be verified within the work but actually constitutes the work. The decentered work constitutes a relational dynamic between the viewer's legitimate demands and the artist's displacement of them in order to coproduce another form of knowledge. Ingrid Luche's renunciation, Maurizio Cattelan's appropriations and Jonathan Monk's desperate acts[6] (I will come back to these later) put the artist in a position of not knowing. The work here is identified with the work of grieving undertaken conjointly by the artist and the viewer. This grieving is the first step towards what would be "the development of new types of art for which there is no division between emission and reception, composition and interpretation."[7]

Before we go any further, however, a little clarification is called for: of course, art began emancipating itself from expectations[8] and forming participatory pacts with viewers a long time before the '90s. Today, however, the viewer is no longer being asked to "fill in" the "open" work, to act as a zealous collaborator seeking to fulfil the program prepared by the artist. No, the goal now is much more dynamic: it is that viewers should produce the work by using the elements

---

[6] One could also mention Thierry Hauch's imitations in his *Pauline* series of videos (1996-1999): on two monitors placed in such a way that it is impossible to take in both screens at the same time, we see, on the one hand, the artist reproducing the gestures of a little girl whom he sees on a screen, and, on the other, the opposite situation: the young girl imitating the artist in his kitchen. The artist always seems off the pace, repeating things approximately and belatedly.

[7] PierreLévy, *L'intelligence collective. Pour une anthropologie du cyberespace*, (Paris: La Découverte, 1997).

[8] See Walter Benjamin's analysis of the rupture brought about by "mechanical reproduction [which] for the first time in world history […] emancipates the work of art from its parasitical dependence on ritual." "The Work of Art in the Age of Mechanical Reproduction," *Illuminations*, (Glasgow: Fontana, 1977), p. 226. See also the different stages in the conquest of autonomy identified by Rainer Rochlitz in *Subvention et subversion*, (Paris: Gallimard, 1994), p. 33-34.

proposed to them.[9] This shatters the belief in a closed object, in a unity that, in the best modernist tradition, celebrates the coherence of form and content. It casts doubt on the traditional reading of media.

To upset the identification of the work with its material form, effecting a shift in reception which would take into account the visual result without however identifying it with the reality of the work—this is what is at stake in Cornelia Parker's *Pornographic Drawings* (1996). What is the nature of Parker's pornography? It has less to do with representation than with the process of realization and reception. For the only pornographic thing about these clumsy drawings is what we may learn about the ink used to make them: it is based on iron oxide from censored porn videos. No pornography can be detected on the level of representation, but it does seep into the support and shifts the viewer's attention away from the visual result and on to the process of making. It is in the way it insinuates itself into the viewer's perceptive awareness that the piece partakes of pornographic seduction. The drawing itself, which is beyond any question of success or failure, and is contaminated by its own procedure, is valid only as the ultimate trace of a process. The trace is consubstantial with the work, but is not in itself sufficient justification for it.

---

[9] The viewer is free to pick up and use the guitars and other musical equipment in Rirkrit Tiravanija's *Rehearsal Studio (Untitled/One Revolution per Minute)*.

Reevaluating media: the underperformance of contemporary photography

This is all worlds away from the huge and luxurious ciba-chromes of Noritoshi Hirakawa's *Virtue in Vice* series (1997), in which young women strike up perfectly neutral poses in front of American churches. There is no sign of virtuosity in the framing. The artist's sole concern is to convey the importance of moment, the effect of which is to make his models seems remote and lost, so that our gaze have to strain after them a bit. There is no sign of a little scandal to back up the promise of the title. Nothing, that is, except in the challenge laid down to our belief in the indicial and analogic virtues of photography. The inevitably deceptual dynamic of these grandiloquent pieces is to give nothing away. They are superb demonstrations of the inadmissible status of photography, its inability to show its underlying motivations. In this case, the models all have a vibrator between their legs. Here, then, we can make out the strategy of these decentered works, whose scope is no longer limited to their visual result. The work is not the photograph that we see before us. Like the vibrator, it is contained by the photograph, not revealed by it. The decept demands that we reevaluate the photographic medium, whose performative ambitions are exposed for what they are. The purported coming together of photographic reality (that which is shown and attested by the real) and psychic reality (what we know) is denied: the visual result rules it out. This prohibition or failing of expectations makes us aware of the desire for the artwork (that of the viewer deprived of their traditional voyeur's position) that is here left unsatisfied. Supposedly identifiable with the photograph (which is by nature vicious), the work (which is virtuous, because deceptive) eludes us. Photography as a contemporary practice asserts its own underperformance. By exposing its own vacuity, it demands that the viewer apprehend it not in terms of images but in terms of activity.

The contemporary photographic deficit is also in evidence in *Three Inches* (1997), a series of photographs of a tattooed index finger by Douglas Gordon. The idea was as follows: to mark on another person's body, their index finger (a particularly judicious choice which alludes to the indicial functioning of the work and to the indicial definition of photography) a sign recalling a traumatic childhood, associated with the regulation maximum length of a knife blade—three inches, or the size of the palm, so that, if blows are dealt they will not reach the adversary's heart. The photographs reaffirm and reproduce the double work of indexing the tattoo and the trauma. The blackened finger shows the traces of the trauma, which is itself the psychic trace of an experience, and these are both indexed by the photograph, which is thus unable to claim artwork status. As the ultimate side product, Gordon's deceptual photograph is but an art object responding to economic imperatives, but it cannot be identified with the absent work. Acting like a screen memory, it here denies the supremacy of the visual result and maintains the gap needed by the always decentered work.

Invented in the 19th century, photography becomes a contemporary practice once it begins to signal its own under-performance. Underperformance: the reference to body art is

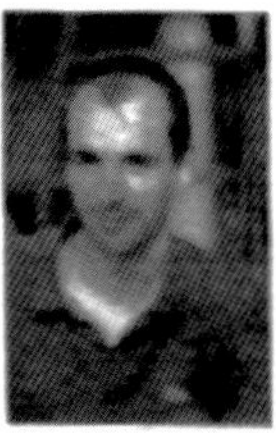

Pierre Joseph

32 ans, né à Caen.

28 avenue Bellevue
06100 Nice
Tel: 0493515513

Formation

- Baccalauréat maths et sciences de la nature, 1984.
- Stage de maquettiste dans l'agence Grafibus en 1985
- DNSEP, diplôme national superieur d'enseignement plastique, Ecole des Beaux-arts de Grenoble, 1989.
- Deux stages à l'ENSAD. Atelier d'image informatique 2D et 3D, 88 et 89.

Expérience professionnelle

- Expositions en France et à l'étranger de mon travail d'artiste: photo, sculpture vivante, installation. 1989/1998.
- Dans le cadre d'une résidence d'artiste de 3 mois au Japon: prise de contact avec l'entreprise japonaise KS (visite de la chaine de montage, participation au contrôle qualité dans un des ateliers), 1997.
- Ouvrier peintre N1 P1 à temps partiel, 1993/1994.
- Travail saisonnier dans l'entreprise de parfum Roger et Gallet (contrôle qualité), 1983.

Langues

- Anglais parlé
- Initiation au japonais

Loisirs

- Mer, montagne pour profiter aussi bien des paysages que des sports qu'on y pratique.

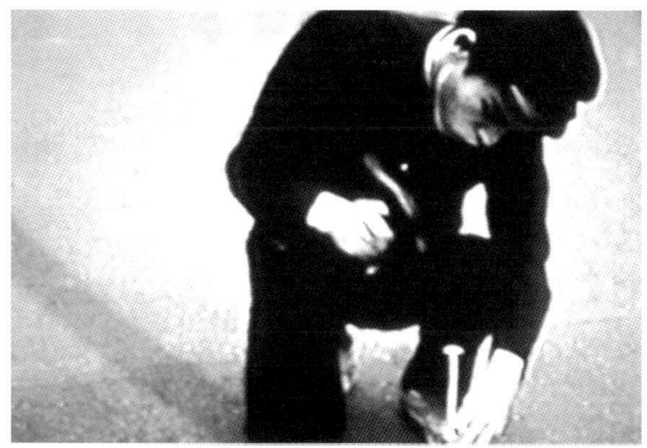

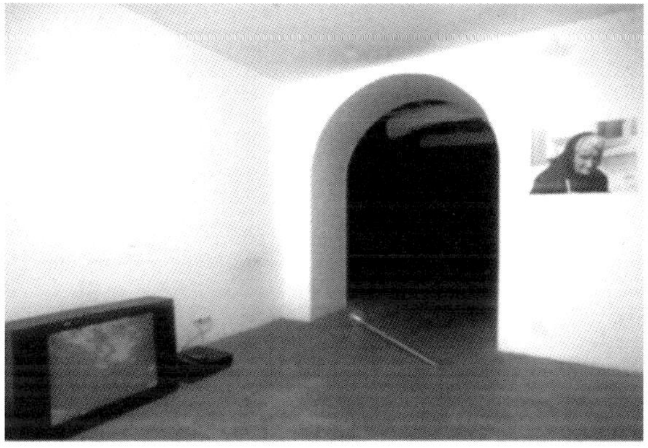

Pierre Joseph: *Influences 4*, 1998
computer print, plastic-coated polychoc
Courtesy Air de Paris

Pierre Joseph: *Curriculum vitae*, 1998
computer print, plastic-coated polychoc
Coll. part.

significant. Ironically present in the work of Douglas Gordon, it manifests photography's acknowledged inability to compete with the absolutely contemporary, *live* dimension of the performer. Already, in 1972, André Cadéré used photography to trick Harald Szeemann, who had made his participation in Documenta conditional on his coming to Kassel on foot. Cadéré in fact made the journey by train, but got off along the way to have himself photographed in the pose of the walker that he was supposed to be (*Le Marcheur de Kassel*, 1972). Here photography deceived the commissioner and failed the expectations of physical performance inherited from body art. The same practice is adopted by Made in Eric in his *Supplément d'information* series (1995) of carefully staged photographs where we see the body/object of the artist serving as, variously, a swing, a pair of briefs or a hedge—in other words, acting out for the camera situations that are not a part of the artist's regular practice, at the risk of discrediting his global project. A spin-off designed for the market, contemporary photography recreates the work but cannot constitute it.

The action of the viewer: inventing contemporaneity

Here, it becomes impossible to judge a work in terms of its visual form. Indeed, to do so would be the sign of a tedious, indolent misunderstanding and could only lead to the verdict inevitably leveled at these contemporary practices, i.e. that they are distinctly lacking in formal accomplishment.[10] It is this sacrali-

[10] The deceptual work is a work without content or form, which ipso facto shatters modernist criteria and other glosses on the necessary and subtle relation between form and content, be it a matter of constructive opposition or harmonious matching.

zation of formal resolution, of form as the ultimate incarnation and token of a work's success or failure, as an obsolete criterion of aesthetic judgment, that the deceptual work refused to acknowledge, engaged as it is in its own process of *formation*.

The decept stands as the condition of the displacement of certitudes, of the questioning of perceptual expectations. The strategy aims to problematize the uncomfortable position of the viewer, who on one side is confined by aesthetic tradition to intervening after the event—after the production of the object— and, on the other, is comforted by his own a priori conceptions —reception precedes the work whose role it is to justify expectations. However, the deceptual work does not honor this contract. Rather than making it possible to come and verify our preconceptions, or asking the viewer to make it complete, it requires the invention of another temporality: the contemporaneity of contemporary art. Deceptual art is thus the "implementation" of a contemporary relation to art. It implies, in other words, an acceptance of the idea that the project of contemporary art can be to question "the contemporary," a matter of time; inventing a relation involving improvisation which is as much a mode of communication as of poetic creation.

As dancers well know, improvising does not mean honoring the cult of spontaneity, but developing one's receptiveness, attentiveness and reactivity. Improvising becomes the mode of reception-creation whereby the viewer is able to experience the constitutive project of the work. When Pierre Huyghe conceives his *Mobile TV*, a TV channel, he does not present a self-contained work, but makes the conditions of realization available to the viewer. What is to be seen does not constitute the work but presents the possibility of its implementation, from the technical equipment to the various authorizations. The work does not preexist the viewer; it requires that the viewer act as coproducer using the resources it makes available. It comes into being in the action of the viewer, an action that replaces the training of the gaze on a *form* (the work-object) with the *formation* of the work. It follows that "the form of the contemporary work extends beyond its material form, it is a linking element, a principle of dynamic agglutination [...] Looking at contemporary artistic practices, it is more appropriate to speak of 'formations' than of 'forms': in opposition to a self-enclosed object sealed by a style or a signature, current art shows that form exists only in the encounter..."[11]

The practice of learning

As a strategy, the decept is essential to such an encounter's mode of artistic relation and, indeed, experience. "When doxic propositions happen to correspond to the objects they concern, satisfaction (aesthetic pleasure) is guaranteed. When they do not, the feeling is one of disappointment. This disappointment is the second element characterizing the state of contemporary art. For this disappointment is active, it shows up the expectations that have been let down. The negative version of the experience tells us about what was expected. It is then, and only then, as if to reestablish the 'true' meanings that appear to be absent from these

---

[11] Nicolas Bourriaud, *L'Esthétique relationnelle, op. cit.* p. 21.

'disappointing' works, which I shall call 'deceptual,' that we see the emergence of the traits whereby the person expecting something comes to state it."[12] It is time, then, for a deceptual art, a dynamic art, a critical revealer of expectations, beliefs and other habits: novelty, universality, originality, authenticity, a message...[13]

1995, Jonathan Monk stands in an airport concourse with placards bearing the names of Andy Warhol, Marcel Duchamp and Jackson Pollock. Looking beyond the ironic self-portrait aspect,[14] what this *mise-en-scène* revealed was the deceptual element at the heart of the artistic experience: the artist waiting, in the position of the receiver, searching for a signature—the metaphor of a demand that cannot be met because no one will come, or at least, not those who are expected, known. This is the edifying fable of a misunderstanding, of disappointed hopes for a return to the past, a scenario that seems to be constantly repeated in the stereotyped relation that the viewer, but also the critic, all too readily cultivates with contemporary practices which they judge disconcerting, at best hermetic and at worst null and void. For it is said that there is now a complete divorce between the public and contemporary art, a break attributed to the artist's obsession with de-defining art,[15] with testing its autonomy, with conducting his experiments while ignoring the

---

[12] Anne Cauquelin, *Petit traité d'art contemporain*, (Paris: Le Seuil, 1996), p. 51. See also p. 52-81 and 106-109.

[13] Cf. Anne Cauquelin, *op. cit.* and Rainer Rochlitz, *L'Art au banc d'essai*, (Paris: Gallimard, 1998), p. 284.

[14] In the series *Waiting for Famous People*.

[15] "The De-definition of Art"—the title of a book by Harold Rosenberg—refers to the modernist dynamic of constantly transgressing the limits of the art concept. Contemporary art can be seen as radicalizing this transgression of the frontiers of art. See *L'Art au banc d'essai. Esthétique et critique, op. cit.*, p. 382-386, and *Subvention et subversion. Art contemporain et argumentation esthétique, op. cit.*, p. 36-39.

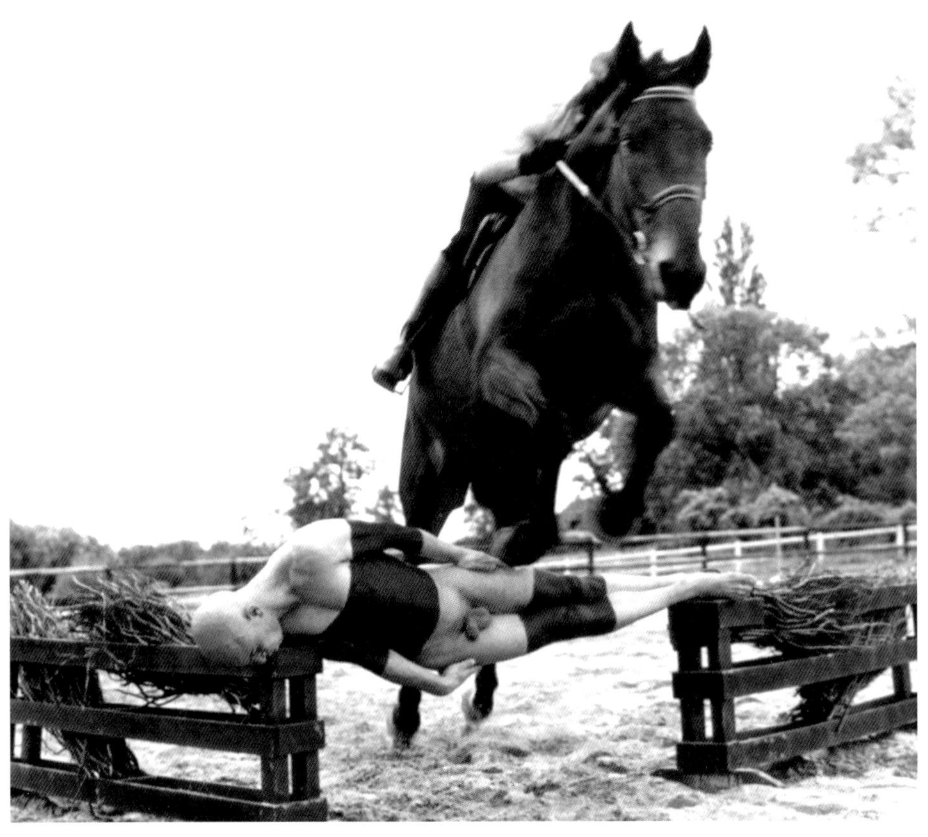

Made in Eric: *Supplément d'information*, 1995
60 x 60 cm
courtesy Made in Eric

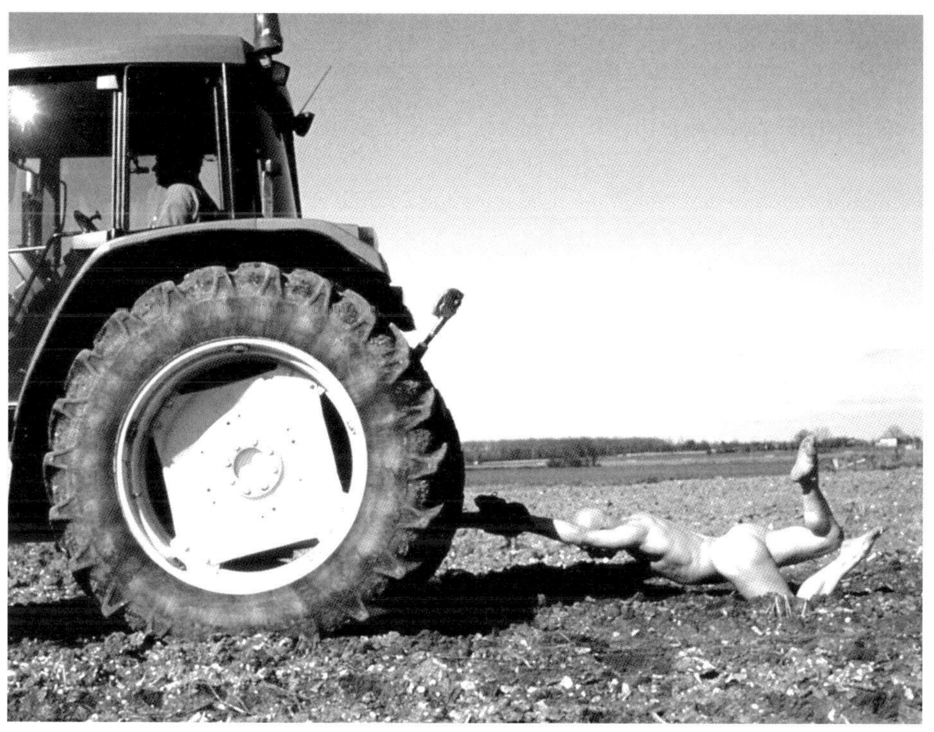

Made in Eric: *Supplément d'information*, 1996
80 x 100 cm
courtesy Made in Eric

conditions of reception, with seeking—and this is what interests us here—to undermine the beliefs of the doxa. At the risk of leaving his audience way behind.[16] Worse, "his [the artist's] provocations are perhaps the flip side of an instrumental conception of art that has failed: having tried in vain to act on social reality by pushing for a social utopia, the artist is in a sense punishing the public for its insensitivity, by disappointing it."[17] Let us recapitulate: failure, vanity, utopia, punishment, disappointment. A dire program, portrait of the artist as bogeyman or avenger. Contemporary art? A huge plot against the public. Contemporary practices? Punitive expeditions. For, "recognized and promoted by the institutions created for that purpose, innovative works no longer perform their function exclusively by virtue of their cognitive content, their importance and their authenticity, as identified by the arguments put forward by critics. They also perform that function in the absence[18] of cognitive, critical content, in the absence of any authenticity and even in the knowingly orchestrated absence of any interest."[19] Point made. The verdict is crushing.

The purported autism of the contemporary artwork, attacked as it is for its refusal to meet public expectations, for its supposed intractability to criticism, might then be seen to authorize the return of idiosyncratic judgment as a last resort in the conflictual

[16] For Pierre Bourdieu, this risk is insurmountable: "As the autonomy of cultural production increases, so does the time needed for the works to win the public over to the norms for their perception, which they themselves introduce (most of the time in opposition to the critics)," *Les Règles de l'art*, (Paris: Le Seuil, 1992), p. 76.
[17] Rainer Rochlitz (1998), *op. cit.*, p. 383.
[18] Italics the author's.
[19] Rainer Rochlitz (1998), *op. cit.*, p. 380-381.

process of reception. Since they seem impervious to criticism, these deceptive works are held responsible for a liberal aesthetic founded on the "relativity of tastes," if only because of their incapacity to comply with the diktats of criteriology.

Here we have the uncomfortable sensation of seeing the same old scenario being played out once again: contemporary practices are blacklisted while stereotyped critical practices and aesthetic theories are maintained. True, it is fair to draw attention to the dangers of idiosyncratic judgment, and there is an urgent need to insist on the need to reinvent an aesthetic, but how can one go on justifying this criteriological reflex? We really do need to analyze this critical pusillanimity, this inability of criticism to be as contemporary as the artistic practices it believes itself duty-bound to examine. "For while critical curiosity will always be important, the role of 'discoverer' or 'advocate' has become the fig leaf hiding the intellectual impotence of critics when it comes to playing their articulating role [...] it seems to me that this is due to a deep and mutual dissatisfaction concerning the hierarchization and division of labor obtaining between the artist and the critic with regard to what has become the most challenging art of the present."[20]

[20] Jean-Christophe Royoux, "Qu'est-ce que la critique d'art contemporain? Plaidoyer pour une 'pédagogie du projet'," *Pratiques*, no. 6, Presses Universitaires de Rennes, spring 1999. In 1995 Anne Cauquelin wrote: "It would seem that the criteria by which, not so long ago, we were able to recognize objects as artworks are no longer appropriate to what we now have before us. We have run out of signs of recognition. No doubt this means that we need to reconsider our habitual propositions, the ones to which we are so accustomed that they seem self-evident to us. Again, I am not talking about erroneous opinions that can generally be attributed to the philistinism (if not the stupidity) of the public, but the whole apparatus, the overall system of our beliefs in something as art, a system which is adhered to by all, from the most learned critic to the humblest of viewers." *Petit traité d'art contemporain, op. cit.* p. 13.

Perhaps this too is the project of a deceptual contemporary art: the invention of a critical discourse (and not critical novelty for its own sake), of a form of viewer reception, of an artistic experience as part of the coproduction of the work.

By playing with the position of the supposed subject of knowledge, artist and viewer are now defining the contemporaneity of artistic experience, and indeed practice. Both must ignore what they already know, what relates to past knowledge. The expectation of novelty[21] is constantly let down by current practices. In 1996 Maurizio Cattelan duplicated the installations of Paul-Armand Gette and John Armleder, presenting them next to the originals (*Cabines de bains*). In 1997, he cloned new works by Carsten Höller and exhibited the copies in an adjacent gallery (*Moi-même, Soi-même*). With these reproductions, which coexist with their models and were presented in the same time and space, the artist was undermining the originality of the critique of novelty as formulated in the remakes of Elaine Sturtevant and Mike Bidlo and the appropriations of Sherrie Levine. By identifying the reappropriation of works and gestures of his predecessors, the artist breaks down any hierarchy between the reproducible work-object (the installations) and the procedure (the appropriationist gesture), thereby undermining our reading of the work. We have here not only a renunciation of the originality of the signature, of authorial status, of the expression of a subjectivity and other elements, all of which have been sufficiently analyzed by art historians for

---

[21] "The new is no longer a criterion, except perhaps for retarded detractors of modern art who see in the hated present only what their traditionalist culture has taught them to loathe in the art of yesteryear." Nicolas Bourriaud, *L'Esthétique relationnelle, op. cit.*, p. 11.

there to be no need to go over these issues again here, but also a brilliant statement of the unacceptability of the belief in a Darwinian logic of artistic practices. Cattelan's work cannot be reduced to either the material form of the installations he reproduced or the process, the gesture he repeated, but instead invents the utopian coming together of these two elements in an act of mourning for history. It is not a matter of revising or denying history, on the contrary, but of neutralizing it within an open-ended conception, of preferring a relational dynamic: the enlightened recycling of contemporary practices.

Thus, to assume that the deceptual artwork is unhitched from critical judgment is a misapprehension. On the contrary, it leads viewers to a new exigency, frees them from judgments based on its form, or formal accomplishment—this being naturally disappointing because the issue now is its contemporaneity. "What, as I see it, defines the contemporary, our experience of which is constantly renewed by the relation to art, is an essential closeness to childhood. Consequently, to make contemporaneity the condition of an experience means constantly and repeatedly putting ourselves in the position of learning to speak of this birth of which it is the symptom. More radically, one could say, with the philosopher Giorgio Agamben, that our skill at having this experience depends on our capacity to maintain ourselves at the level of this exigency—learning a language that we do not yet speak—which characterized childhood."[22] Now, this idea of learning is central

---

[22] Jean-Christophe Royoux, "Qu'est-ce que la critique d'art contemporain? Plaidoyer pour une 'pédagogie du projet'," *loc. cit.*

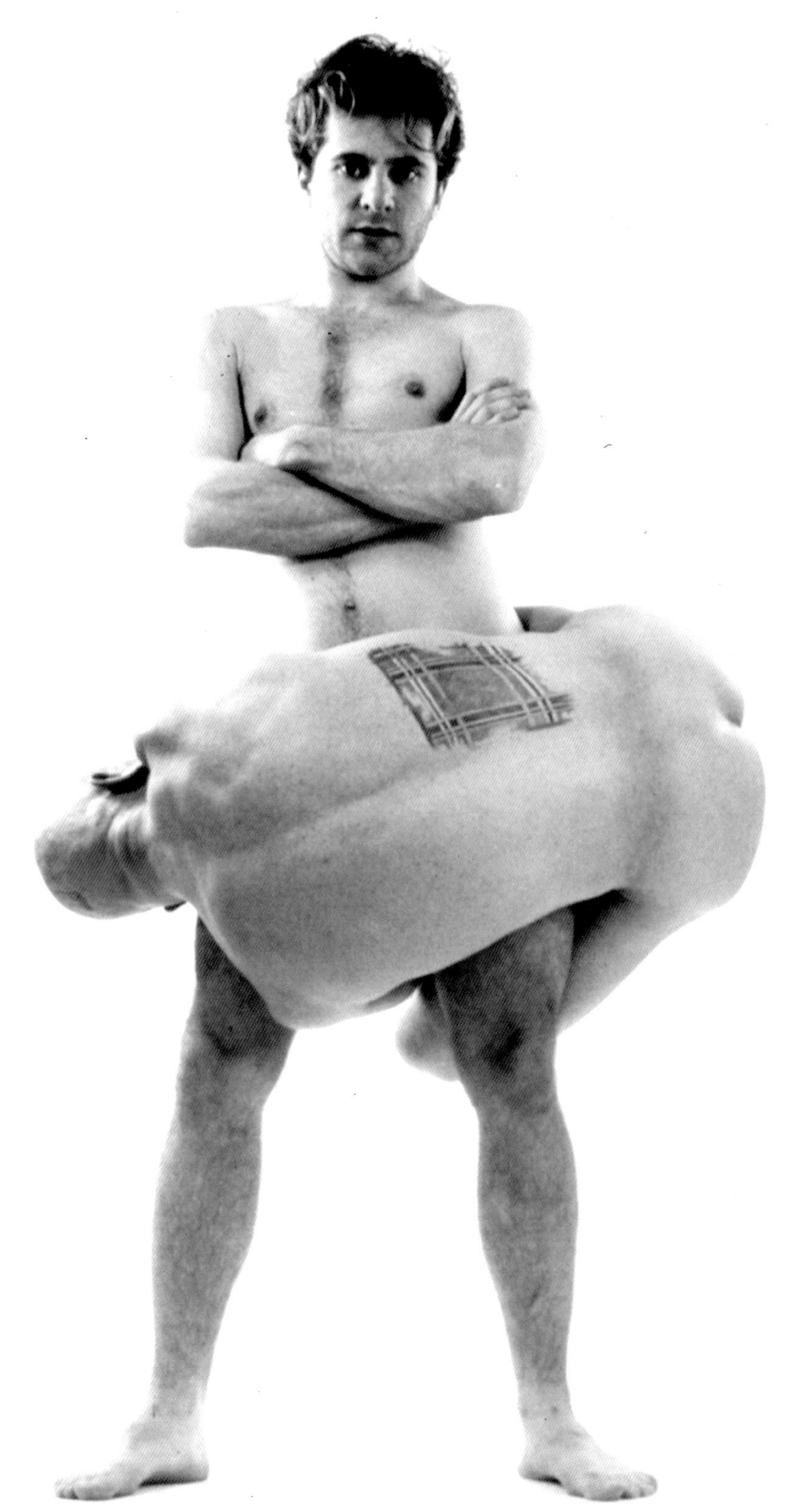

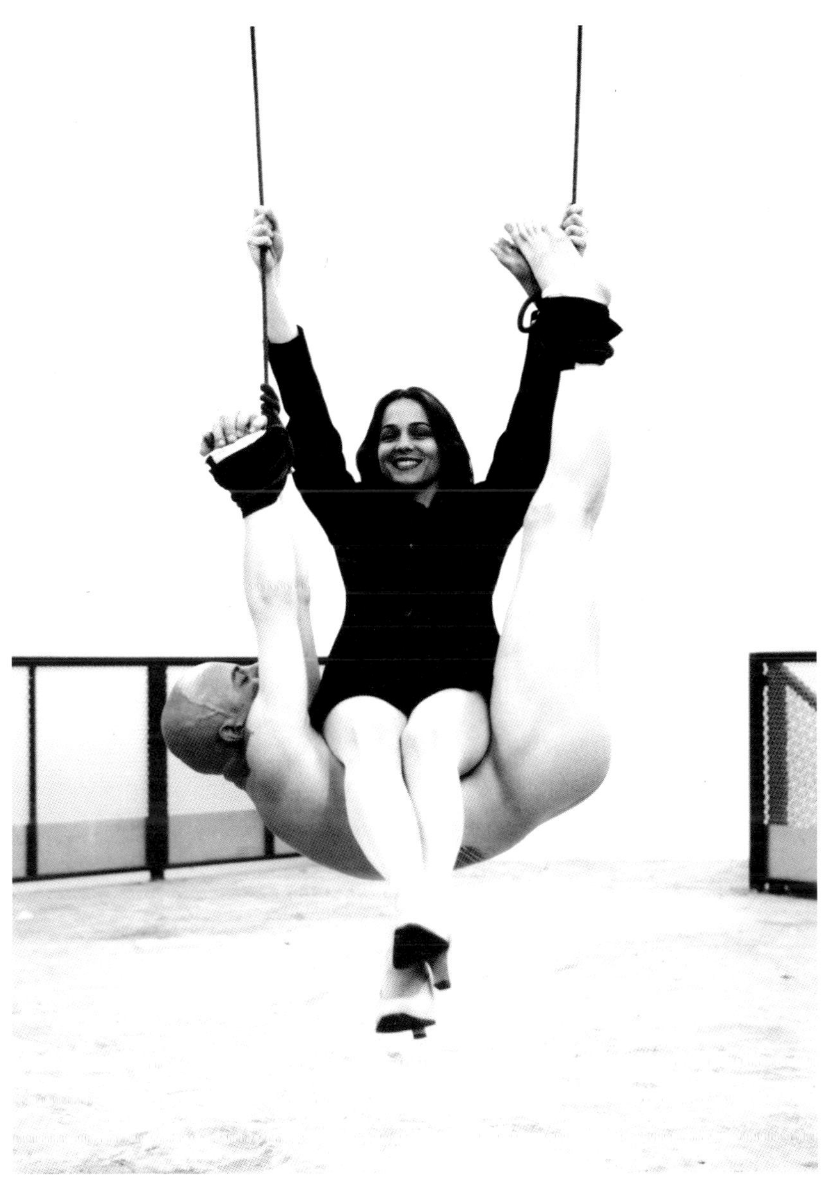

Made in Eric: *Supplément d'information*, 1996
120 x 60 cm
Courtesy Made In Eric

Made in Eric: *Supplément d'information*, 1996
62 x 42 cm
Courtesy Made In Eric

to the debate on contemporary art, as an artistic experience undergone by artists who renounced their sovereignty long ago. One thinks, of course, of the work done by Pierre Joseph in 1998, on his return from Japan. Judging by the exhibition, his trip is a question mark placed over what the artist knows. For him, the journey was an opportunity to experience learning as a way of relating to the world, whether through the characters of hiragana (a new language) or through baseball. The various elements in the exhibition throw what the artist knows into crisis, show him accepting a form of inadequacy. But there is nothing romantic about this position: all we have is a series of pieces of work to be undertaken as the different stages in acquiring knowledge, with all the tedium and difficulties that this implies—those, for example, of drawing from memory a map reflecting his experience and showing all the places he frequented. The hypothetical map here becomes a personal plan, the trajectory of an experience that includes omissions and other failures. An even more radical production of lack is the artist's *Curriculum vitae* (1998), detailing his education, professional experience, language skills and hobbies, and complete with a photograph. With this CV, the artist not only declines and details the position of the supposed subject of knowledge, and accepts his failures, but also implies that the contemporaneity of art is the constitutive project of the artistic experience. By abandoning the power discourse tied to the mastery of knowledge, the artist undermines the balance of power that the viewer is prepared to maintain; he rejects the violence of hierarchy. And thus he frees individual behavior from the influence of models and poses the conditions of a truly democratic artistic experience.

No, the deceptual work is not a challenge that seeks to punish viewers for their incompetence, to ride roughshod over critical judgment and to assert the lofty superiority of an artist figure who is used to dealing with public contempt. For it is here that contemporary art's need to continually go beyond the given definitions finds its imperative to move beyond aesthetic criteriology, the refusal of the a-priori as a mode of reception. And it is here that the role of the critic needs to be reconsidered. For criticism cannot go on hiding behind its certainties or its decidedly inadequate practices. Instead of seeing the deceptual work as an affront, a rejection of its well-rehearsed discourse, it would do better to seek its own legitimacy elsewhere than in the function of accompanying, commentating and reviewing the work. The time has gone when criticism was called on to produce an endorsing discourse on the work, to endow it with its hidden meaning, to reveal it. What is required now is to coproduce the pedagogical project of a truly contemporary art, to support the political goal of a truly interactive dynamic: the invention of democracy. Not to meet the demand for a finished product is to reject the totalitarian capitalist logic of profitability, to counter the imperatives of zero-defect and other artistic ISOs. "This necessary lack, this fragility that is inherent in the art of our time, is what defines the contemporary, not only as that which has a privileged relation to actuality, to the present, to the now, but as a specific quality: in art, the contemporary is a way of considering attentiveness and receptiveness to the nascent, to the incipient, as the center, the central concern or specific project of art itself."[23]

[23] *Idem.*

By putting himself in a position of not knowing, of learning—
and not of refusing to know—the artist treats the fragile
conditions of 'initiation' and 'reception' together on the same
level." Thus the dynamic, project, issues and subject of the
deceptual work are to be found in this relation, and not only in
a reception and response that occur after the event.

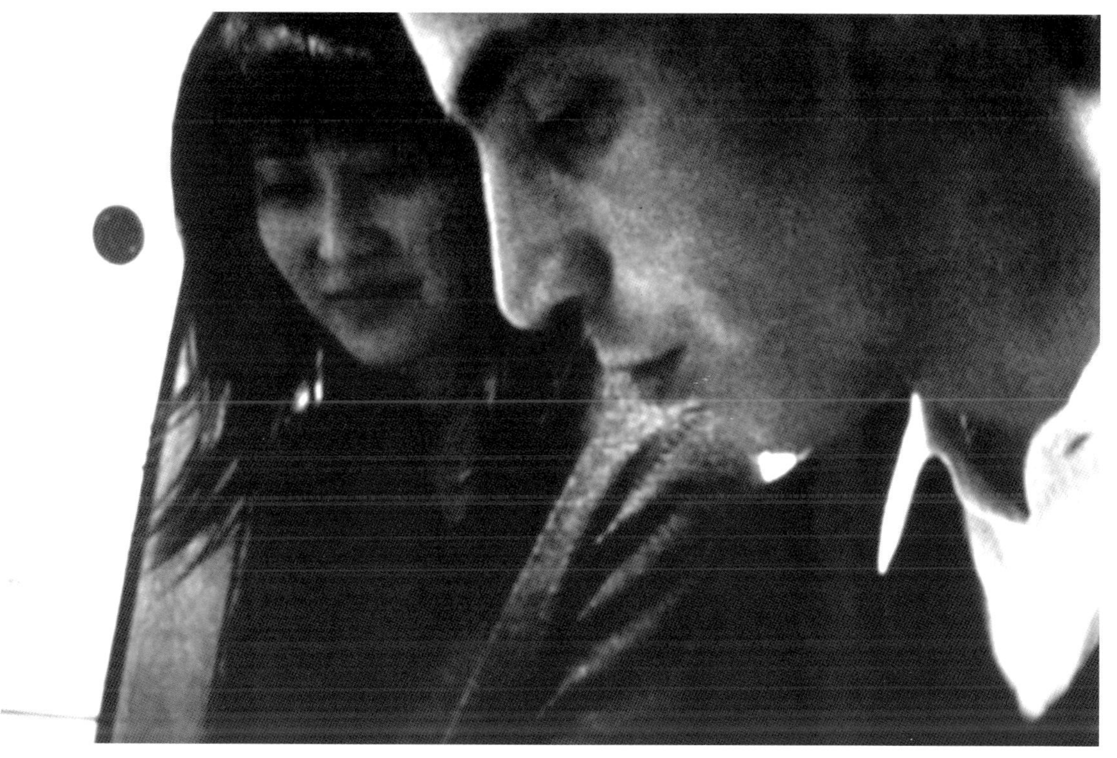

Pierre Joseph: *Akane*, 1997
video 32mn

Courtesy Air de Paris

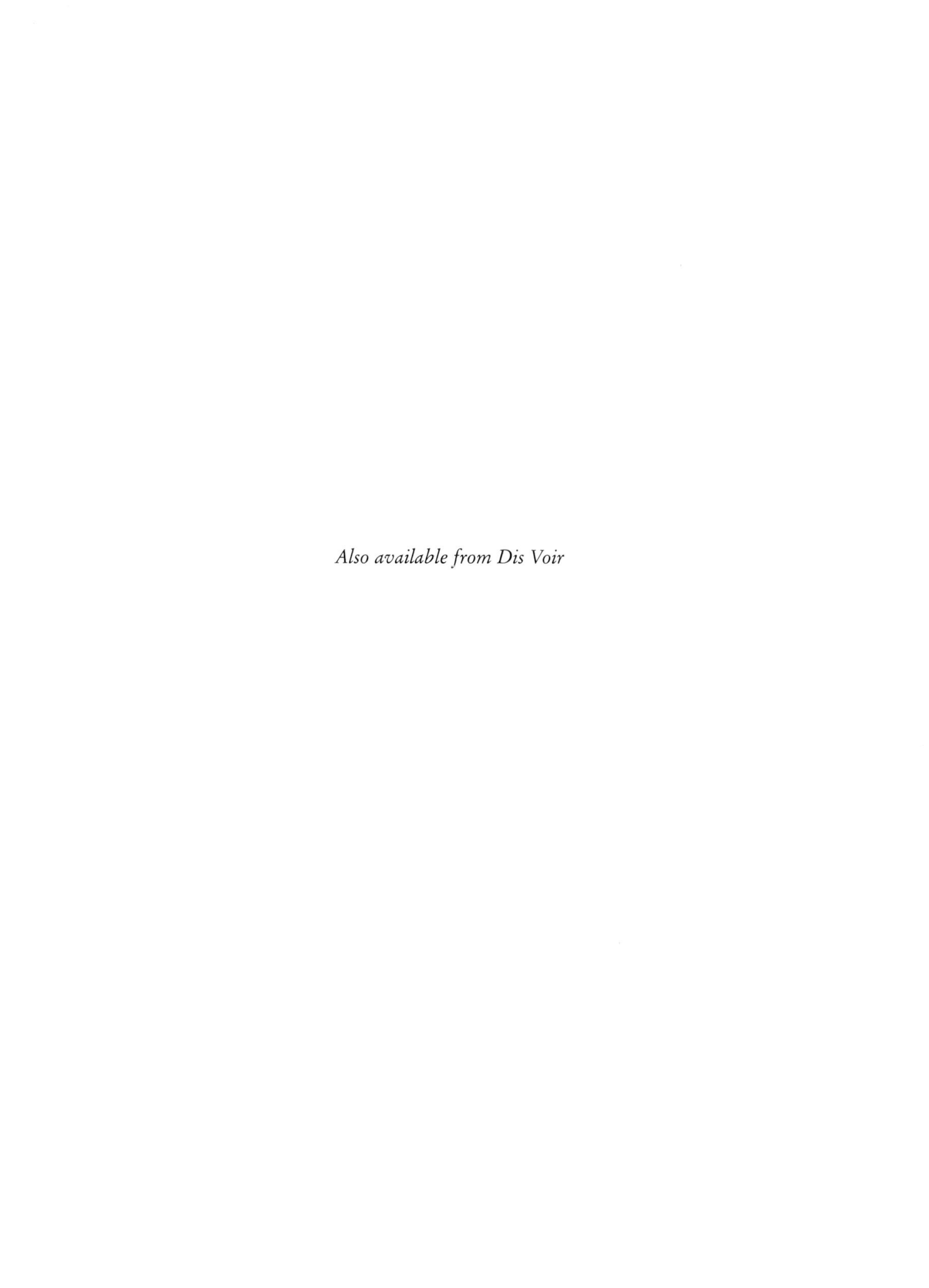

Also available from Dis Voir

LITERATURE/FINE ART/CINEMA

Raúl Ruiz
> *Poetics of Cinema*
> *The Book of Disappearances &*
> *The Book of Tractations*

Peter Greenaway
> *The Falls*
> *Rosa*
> *Fear of Drowning by Numbers*
> *Papers–(Paintings, Collages and Drawings)*
> *The Cook, the Thief, his Wife and her Lover*
> *The Baby of Mâcon*
> *The Pillow Book*

Manoel de Oliveira
> *Angelica*

CINEMA

Jean-Pierre Rehm, Olivier Joyard, Danièle Rivière
> *Tsaï Ming-liang*

Jean-Marc Lalanne, Ackbar Abbas, David Martinez, Jimmy Ngai
> *Wong Kar-wai*

Paul Virilio, Carole Desbarats, Jacinto Lageira, Danièle Rivière
> *Atom Egoyan*

Michael Nyman, Daniel Caux, Michel Field, Florence de Mèredieu, Philippe Pilard
> *Peter Greenaway*

Christine Buci-Glucksmann, Fabrice Revault d'Allonnes
> *Raúl Ruiz*

Yann Lardeau, Jacques Parsi, Philippe Tancelin
> *Manoel de Oliveira*

CHOREOGRAPHY

Paul Virilio, René Thom,
Laurence Louppe,
Jean-Noël Laurenti,
Valérie Preston-Dunlop
*Traces of Dance–
Drawings and
Notations of Choreographers*

ARCHITECTURE

Christian de Portzamparc
Genealogy of forms

DESIGN

Pascale Cassagnau,
Christophe Pillet
*Starck's Kids?
(Beef, Matali Crasset,
Jean-Marie Massaud,
Patrick Jouin, Brétillot/Valette)*

Chloé Braunstein,
Gilles de Bure
Roger Tallon

Charles-Arthur Boyer,
Federica Zanco
Jasper Morrison

Pierre Staudenmeyer, Nadia
Croquet, Laurent Le Bon
Garouste et Bonetti

Philippe Louguet, Dagmar
Sedlickà
Borek Sìpek

Raymond Guidot, Olivier
Boissière
Ron Arad

François Burkhardt, Cristina
Morozzi
Andrea Branzi

ÉDITIONS DIS VOIR:
3, RUE BEAUTREILLIS – F-75004 PARIS
TÉLÉPHONE (33/1) 48 87 07 09
FAX (33/1) 48 87 07 14
EMAIL: DISVOIR@AOL.COM